IMAGES OF AMERICA

AROUND
BALLSTON LAKE

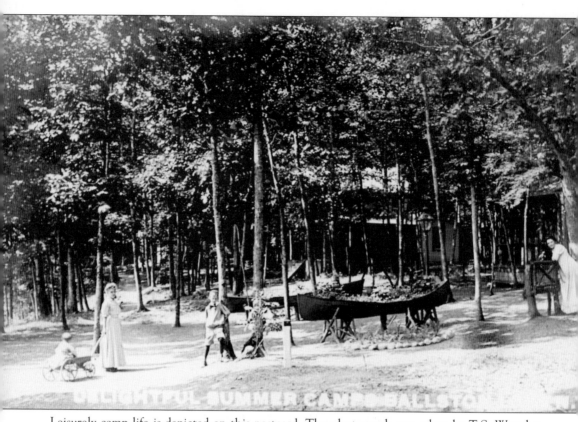

Leisurely camp life is depicted on this postcard. The photograph was taken by T.S. Woosley. Oh! those lazy, hazy days of summer on Ballston Lake.

Cover photograph: Ballston's baseball team poses in 1930. They competed against Round Lake and Scotia. (See page 108.)

IMAGES OF AMERICA

AROUND
BALLSTON LAKE

KATHERINE Q. BRIADDY

ARCADIA

First published 1997
Reissued 2004

Published by Arcadia Publishing,
an imprint of Tempus Publishing Inc.
Portsmouth NH, Charleston SC, Chicago,
San Francisco

Printed in Great Britain

Library of Congress Catalog Card Number: 2004100634

For all general information, contact Arcadia Publishing:
Telephone 843-853-2070
Fax 843-853-0044
E-mail sales@arcadiapublishing.com
For customer service and orders:
Toll-free 1-888-313-2665

Visit us on the Internet at www.arcadiapublishing.com

This book is dedicated to all our ancestors,
who trod the same paths we do,
and to Lewis Sears and Frank Lafforthun,
my inspirations.

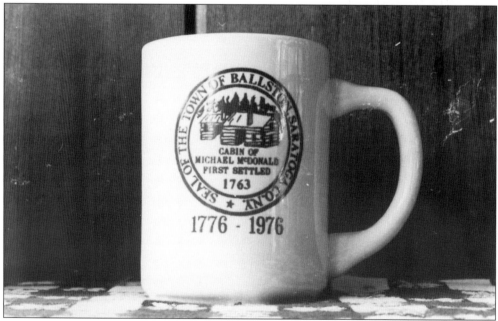

The seal of the Town of Ballston was used during the National Bicentennial celebration on commemorative items.

Contents

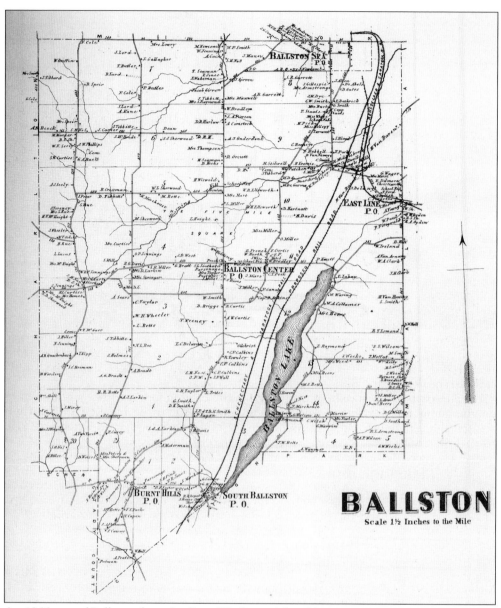

An 1866 map of Ballston, from the S. and D. Beers *Atlas of Saratoga County*, New York (1878).

Introduction

Local history is like a quilt. Small pieces are stitched together to make the whole. So it is with Ballston's history in photographs; each one represents a piece of our history to make a quilt of our mutual heritage.

Ballston derives its name from the Reverend Eliphalet Ball (1722–1797), who is the acknowledged founder. Reverend Ball left Bedford, New York, due to "broils and disputes" with his "old-light" conservative congregation in 1769. Some twenty families from his former flock followed the reverend to the "Five Mile Square," the name given to Ballston at first.

Ballston was set apart from the Kayaderosseras Patent as the "expense allotment"; that is, the sale of the land would help defray the expense of surveying the entire Patent. Reverend Ball was granted 500 acres of land, and he acted as a real estate agent, as well as spiritual advisor.

The settlers barely had time to secure shelter in their log cabins and plant their first crops when news arrived that "blood has been shed at Lexington." Patriotic Ballstonians served in the militia under Lieutenant Colonel James Gordon. Many a Revolutionary War pensioner proudly proclaimed he had witnessed the surrender of Burgoyne.

Ballston was deeply divided during the War for Independence. A hotbed of Tories lived in the northwest part of town, and they continually aided the Redcoats and Tory spies. The most notorious and hated spy was the native, Joe Bettys, known as Ballston's version of Benedict Arnold. Bettys harbored a special vengeance against his patriot neighbors, until he was finally captured and hanged in 1782.

Despite constant vigilance from the soldiers at the Ballston fort, the town was invaded by surprise during the Revolution. The northern portion of town on Middle Line Road was devastated by the British and Mohawk Indians on a cold, moonlit night in October of 1780. Aroused from their beds, the American military leaders and their slaves were captured and taken to Canada. Their houses were plundered and burned, leaving their families in panic. There they remained until peace was declared.

The close of the war brought new growth to Ballston. Advertisements enticed farmers to purchase loamy tracts for farms and orchards. New industrial activity spawned mills and tanneries on streams. Stagecoach lines bustled with travelers to the famed Ballston Springs.

Ballston originally encompassed what is now the towns of Ballston, Milton, Charlton, Galway, Providence, Edinburgh, and part of Greenfield. In 1788 Ballston received its present boundaries, which are used for the limits of this book.

Saratoga County was formed from Albany County in 1791. The new county seat was built on Middle Line Road. The courthouse and jail were built there and continued there until 1816, when it was burned by escaping prisoners. The county seat was then moved to Ballston Spa.

Horatio Spofford described Ballston in his 1824 *Gazetteer of New York*: "Ballston, a Post-Township of Saratoga County, 23 miles northerly of Albany; bounded N. by Milton, E. by Malta, S. by Half-Moon, and a small part of Schenectady County; W. by Charlton. Its extent is about equal to 5 miles square. The general surface of Ballston is an elevated plain country—an open campaign, agreeably undulated with swells of a moderate height. The soil is principally a strong gravelly loam, with some tracts of sand and of clay. In some parts the loamy tracts are very stony, but taken together the land is productive, and yields grain or grass, though grass is the most natural. For apple orchards it is very excellent, and the fruit is of the best quality for cider. The forest trees are of a lofty growth, and embrace a very great variety of kinds. The loamy lands have deciduous trees; and elm, ash, walnut, oak, maple, beech, birch, and basswood, seem scattered in indiscriminate mixture, as if all found a choice of soil on the same spot. There are some groves of hemlock in the NE. part, on a hardpan of forbidding aspect, probably a low southern extremity of the Palmertown mountain, with a dip under the surface between here and a little N. of Saratoga Springs; and pine is principally confined to the Sandy plains or the marshes, though it slightly speckles the groves of deciduous trees.

Some of the swells of the highest hills rise with a gentle ascent, arable throughout, until their summits may be 200 feet above Long Lake. And from these the view is extensive, and elegantly picturesque. On the E. the Vermont mountains lift their lofty heads and bound a distant view; on the N. are those of Lake George; the distant Kaatsburgs in the S. surmount the nearer Helderbergs, and the eye embraces, from a moderate elevation, an extent and distinctness of view seldom equaled. The farms, farm-houses, fields and forests of the intermediate plains and hills invite to nearer view, and give a lively interest to perspective: nor are these remarks so peculiarly applicable to Ballston, that other towns in the same vicinity deserve no similar detail. The Mourn Kill, a small mill-stream, curves eastward across the northern part, towards the Kayaderosseras creek: and Ballston Lake, or Long Lake, a natural pond of near 4 miles in length and 90 rods wide in some places, extends from the S. line toward the NE. part, a little SE. of the center of the Town. This pond has an outlet, on which are mills. A dreary marsh of considerable extent extends from the lower end of this lake along the outlet, which, from Ballston, passes eastward through Malta, to the Round Lake, thence to the Hudson on the S. boundary of Stillwater. These streams supply a scanty number of mills. The inhabitants are principally farmers, of plain domestic habits, possessing the blessings of industry, temperance, and frugality. Much of their clothing is the joint product of their farms and houses, the most honorable to farmers of any that can be worn. The lands are held by right of soil.

The roads are too numerous to be good, and are principally confined to right lines, the boundaries of surveys. That in the center, leading N. and S. is called the middle-line-road; and there are roads on the E. and W. lines of the Township, called the E. and W. line-roads. There are in this Town, 1 Congregational, 1 Episcopal, 1 Presbyterian, 1 Christian, and 1 Baptist meeting-house. There is also an academy, and 10 school-houses. The court-house and jail were formerly in this town, in a pleasant situation, 2 miles SW of Ballston Spa, but having been burned down a few years since, they are now erected in the latter village, and the 'old Court-House Hill' is hardly a Hamlet. There is small village at the *Academy Hill*, 3 miles S of the Spa, where is the Ballston Post Office and some 20 buildings. The academy is pretty respectable, but like too many of these schools, it makes pedantic smatterers in Latin and Greek, rather than sound English scholars. Population, 2,407; taxable property, $311,178; acres of improved land, 12,392; electors, 412; —1,747 cattle, 522 horses, 3,094 sheep; yards of cloth made in families: 12,060; 2 grist mills, 7 saw mills, 2 fulling mills, 1 carding machine, 1 trip hammer, 3 distilleries, and 1 brewery.—Ballston Spa is in the town of Milton, on the N border of this Town.—The first settlements in this Town were made in 1763, by two brothers of the name of McDonald, from Ireland, one of which lived to 1823."

An economic boom came again in 1831 when the second railroad in New York State was built from Schenectady to Saratoga Springs. Industrialists and farmers benefited from the new rapid transport, which shipped their goods far and wide. The railroad also brought tourists to the pristine lake and springs, and showplace mansions were built for their leisure.

Prior to open hostilities in the Civil War, Ballston served as an integral part of the Underground Railroad. Numerous "holds" for escaping slaves have been uncovered behind chimneys and in basements.

Ballston has gradually been transformed from a chiefly agricultural community to a residential suburb. However, since its very founding, the town has been known for its outstanding apple orchards and family-owned farms. In 1813 it was written that the Ballston apples were "the best quality for cider." So it remains today—the apple tree providing shades of the past.

When Eliphalet Ball first arrived to the land that would bear his name, he found it "covered with forest and deer abounding." How proud he would be of the growth in his township! And, how proud he would be that the townsfolk still honor their heritage.

One
Formative Years

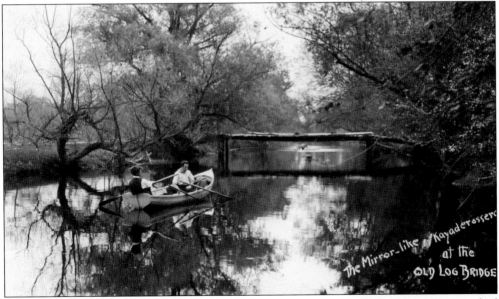

The name "Kayaderosseras" comes from the Native American vocabulary meaning "crooked stream." The area was a favorite hunting ground of the Mohawk tribes. They traveled from their long houses on the Mohawk River to the outlet of Shanantaha (Ballston Lake), then to the Kayaderosseras Creek, and finally to Saratoga Lake. From there, by way of the Fishkill, they reached the Hudson River.

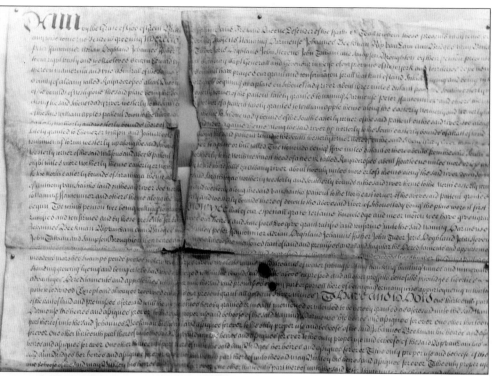

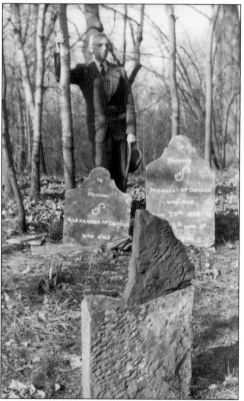

The Kayaderosseras Patent was granted by Queen Anne in 1708. The colonial land grant encompassed what is now Saratoga County and parts of neighboring counties. Over 400,000 acres were given to colonial leaders, although the Mohawks had agreed to sell land for a small farm.

Pictured here are the graves of the McDonald brothers, Michael and Nicholas, who are known as the first "white" settlers in the area. They built a crude log cabin in 1763 and traded with the Mohawks. A tale is told that Eliphalet Ball bought the right to name the town after himself from the McDonald brothers for a gallon of rum. Hundreds of arrowheads have been found near their cabin site. Lewis Sears, eminent former town historian and descendant of the founding families, stands by the graves, which are located on the west shore of Ballston Lake.

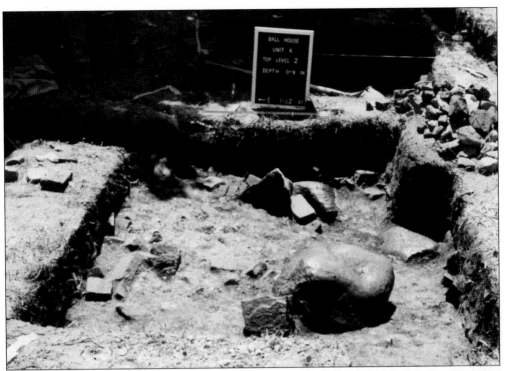

Reverend Eliphalet Ball settled on the east side of Route 50, north of Outlet Road, in 1771. The site is on one the highest elevations in the town. The settlers needed to be on a constant look-out for the Mohawks. A professional archeological dig uncovered spoons, coins, buttons, and numerous other artifacts from his home site. The cabin burned c. 1850.

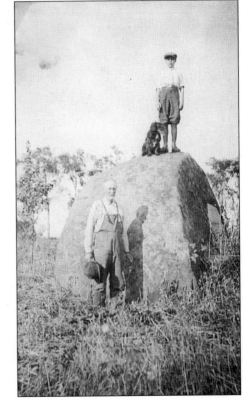

In this image, Edward Leahey stands in front of "Indian Rock" on the east side of Ballston Lake. According to legend, Mohawks captured settlers and tortured them at the rock. The tribes resented the settlers who had built their houses on sacred burial grounds.

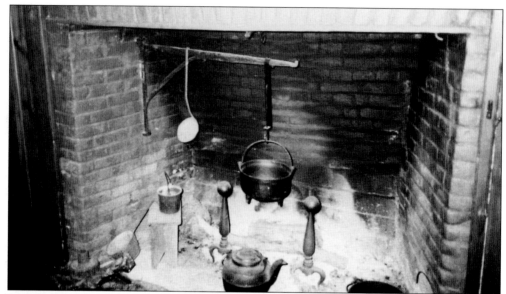

Founding families, who had followed Eliphalet Ball, built log cabins. The typical cabin had beamed ceilings, wide plank flooring, and plastered walls. The fireplace provided warmth and fire for cooking. The earliest houses faced southward in order to protect the family from the northern wind.

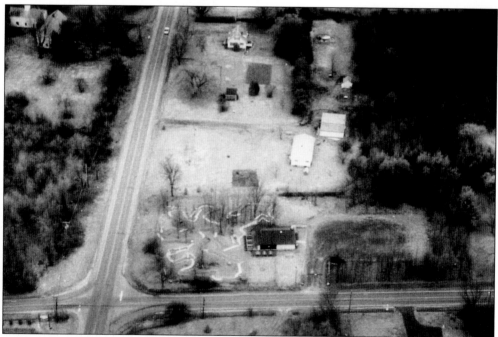

This is an aerial view by Brad Callahan. In 1775 the Ballston Committee of Safety was instructed to build a fort on the corner of Route 50 and Charlton Road. It was built near Ball's log church and the Town Commons. The fort was surrounded by a palisade of oak logs with loop holes for musketry and sentry boxes. The embankments of the fort can still be seen from the air. The settlers complained that the militia made too much noise during their Sabbath services and that they stole their strawberries.

American Patriots from Ballston served in the Albany County Militia, Twelfth Regiment. They complained about the lack of supplies, the hours of drilling, and boredom. Soldiers were to obtain their own guns, which were known as Brown Besses.

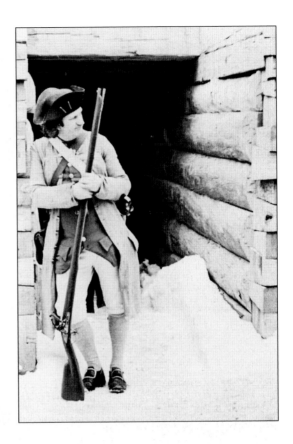

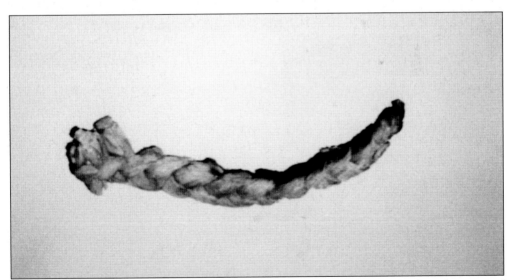

In 1780, three years after the surrender of Johnny Burgoyne at Bemis Heights, the town of Ballston was invaded by British Regulars and Mohawk Indians. The band captured twenty-two Patriots, tomahawked to death Isaac Stow, and burned the houses and barns on the northern portion of Middle Line Road. The Mohawks used hemp-braided torches to light the fires, like this one pictured, which was found in one of the walls of the Jonathan Filer house (see page 81).

13

Received Ballston 21st December 1795 of the Trustees of
the Presbyterian Society in Ballston Five Bushel wheat and
Ten Shilling in full for boarding the Revd Mr Hill Five weeks
and keeping his horse, by the hand of Aaron Nash

       5 Bushel at 17/ £ 2.. 5 –   *Eliphalet Ball*
       Keeping Horse   10 –
                    2.. 15 –
Paid for washing candle   15 –
  & wood   £3.. 10.. 0
Recd the contents of the above £3.. 10 of Messrs Caulkin
                     A. Nash

To The Trustees of the Presbyterian Congregation in Ballston
Gentlemen please to pay To Stephen Ball Four pounds Ten
Shillings and place the Same To my account and you.ll
          Oblidge   yours
                    Ruth Ball

Eliphalet Ball and his second wife, Ruth Beecher
Ball, signed letters to the Presbyterian Society.

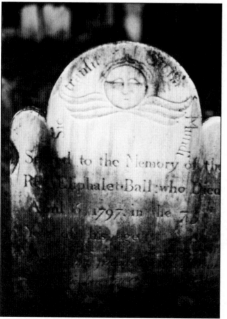

Eliphalet Ball is buried in Briggs Cemetery on
Brookline Road. He died on April 6, 1797, at
age 75. His gravestone is inscribed, "So passes
away the Glory of the World." His inventory of
estate included seventeen chairs, a silver watch,
and one yoke of oxen.

James Gordon was born in 1739 in Antrim, Ireland. He immigrated to America and served in the French and Indian wars. He bought hundreds of acres of land in Ballston and married Eliphalet Ball's daughter, Mary. Gordon was a general in the Revolution and was captured in the 1780 raid. He was held in Canada until he escaped in 1782. He was Ballston's first town supervisor and held numerous political offices on the state and national level. This is a photograph of a miniature. The austere pose comes from the practice of packing the mouth with cotton to compensate for the lack of teeth.

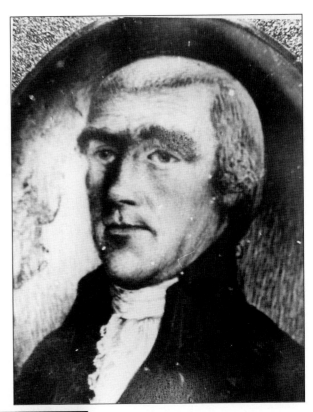

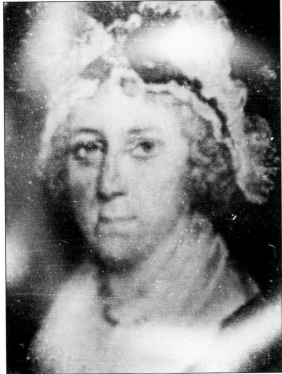

Mary Ball was born in 1753, the daughter of Eliphalet Ball and Elizabeth Von Flamen. She had three brothers, John, Stephen, and Flamen, and a baby sister, Betsey. She married James Gordon on St. Patrick's Day of 1775. Mary gave birth to Melinda and Alexander. She died in 1803, being "carried off by a turn of the Bilious Cholic."

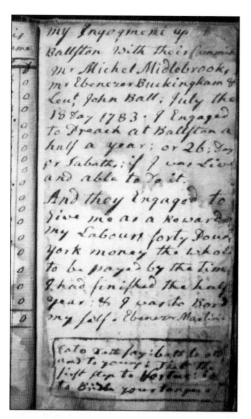

Reverend Ebenezer Martin was the third pastor of the Presbyterian Church. He came to Ball's Town in 1783 and kept a diary during his term. On November 12, he wrote, "I have been much fatigued and nearly broke my neck in trying to heal the measles among the people."

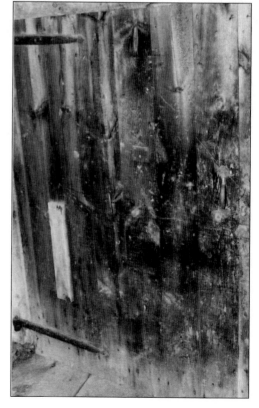

The Red Meeting House was built c. 1780 to replace the original log church. The building was a church, courthouse, and the center of gatherings until 1803, when the congregation built a new church on Charlton and Middle Line Road. After 1803, the Red Meeting House was converted to the Ballston Academy. The meetinghouse was destroyed, but the door still has traces of red paint. It has been written that Alexander Hamilton and Aaron Burr once argued a legal case at the meetinghouse, which was used as the county courthouse. One of the last cases tried there was a woman accused of grand larceny. She was sentenced to be whipped at the "public whipping post." Also, a man was found dead with a wound to the back of his skull. The mystery was investigated at the Red Meeting House, but it remains unsolved.

Two
Ballston Lake

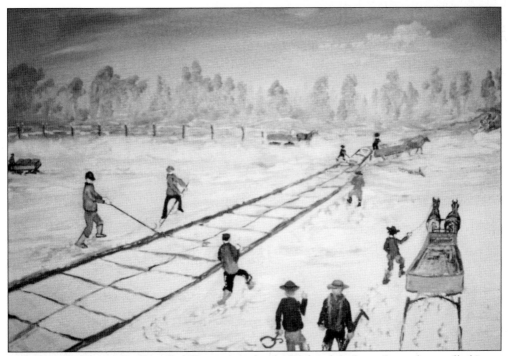

Ballston Lake was originally called Shanantaha by the Mohawk Indians. It was later called Long Lake by the first settlers. Aside from recreational use, the lake provided commercial enterprise, as there was a large ice harvesting operation. This painting, by Edward Sutphen, depicts workers sawing ice cakes, which weighed 300 pounds each. In the 1870s, over 25,000 tons of ice were harvested and sent by railroad to nearby cities.

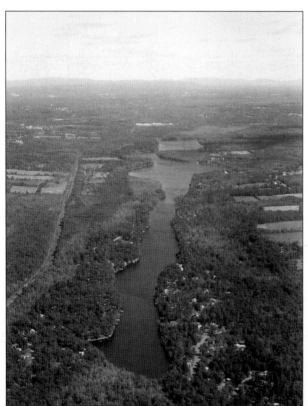

An aerial photograph by Brad Callahan is shown here. Ballston Lake is 3 and 7/10 miles long and varies in depth to 200 feet. It was originally part of the Mohawk River after the glacial age. The lake is known for bass fishing and is on the migratory path of the Great blue herons. Artifacts have been recovered on the banks of this lake, proving early occupancy by Lamoka tribes, 3500 B.C.!

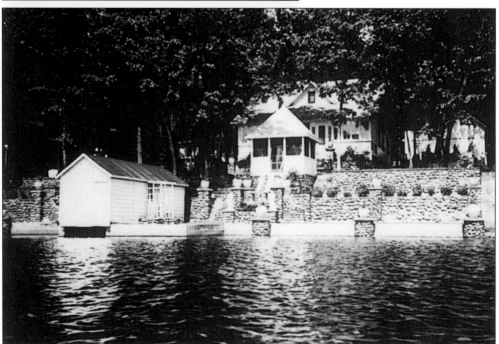

Echo Lodge was built about 1930 at 136 Westside Drive. It is one of the showplaces on the lake. A stone footpath in front of the lakeside homes was a popular walkway.

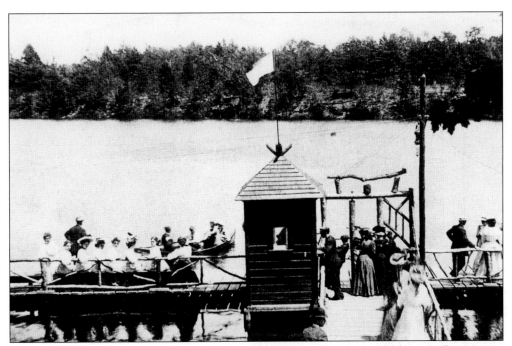

Forest Park was opened in 1904. Boating was popular, and canoes could be rented. A steam-driven boat, called the *Comanche*, provided scenic rides. It was located at 80 Westside Drive.

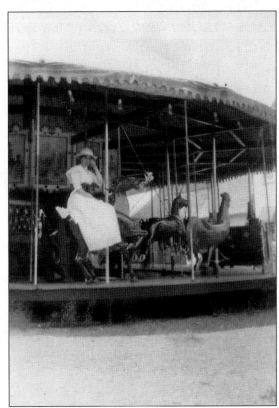

Esther Ruth Mead is pictured here on the Forest Park merry-go-round in 1914. A hurdy-gurdy provided the music, and a ride cost 5¢. The horses had rhinestone collars and eyes, and everyone tried to catch the brass ring for a free ride.

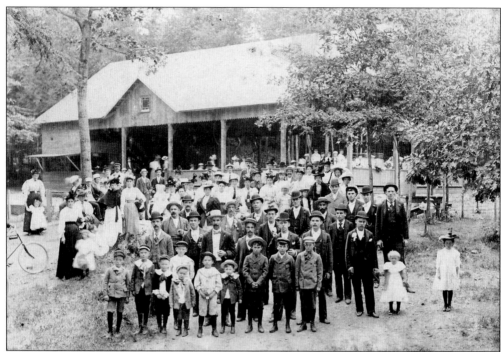

The pavilion at Forest Park was the site of many a romance. The Hemlock stop on the trolley brought folks to Forest Park in the "Moonlight Special" trolley ride. This was the site of picnics, dances, fireworks, and firemen's clambakes.

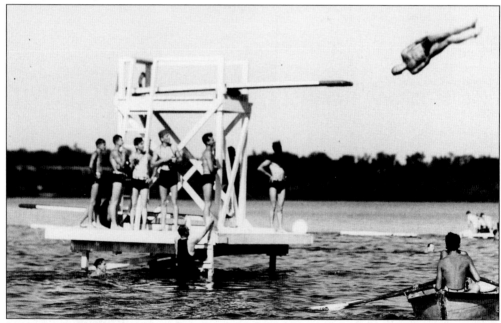

J.B. White established White's Beach in 1932 on the northwest portion of Ballston Lake. White sand was hauled in to build a beautiful beach. There were baseball diamonds, clambake sheds, pony rides, and a place for school picnics. Lifeguards were on duty, and lights out was at midnight. White's Beach was purchased by Harold Spoonogle in 1950.

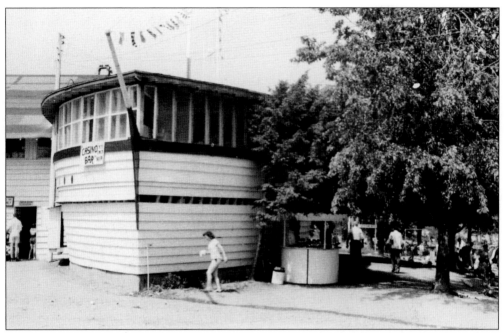

The "boat" house at White's Beach was a place to change into swimming suits. A diner there provided clambakes and barbecues.

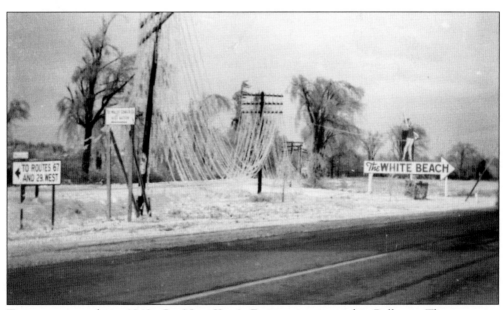

Times were tough in 1940. On New Year's Eve, an ice storm hit Ballston. There was no power, and hence no water from wells for a week. When the power was restored, several fires were ignited.

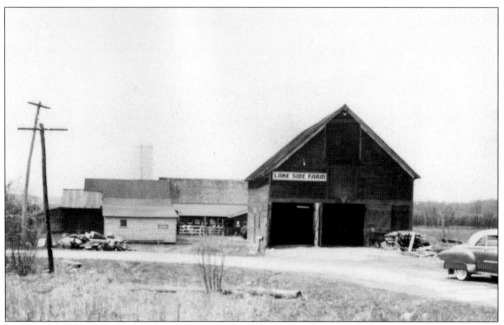

There are many historically significant sites on the east side of Ballston Lake because it was one of the earliest areas of settlement. Dick and Lorraine Pearce bought Lakeside Farm, at Lundy's corners, in 1949. Their children, Lisa, Richard, and Jeff, assist with the business. Lakeside is known as the farm that originated apple cider donuts.

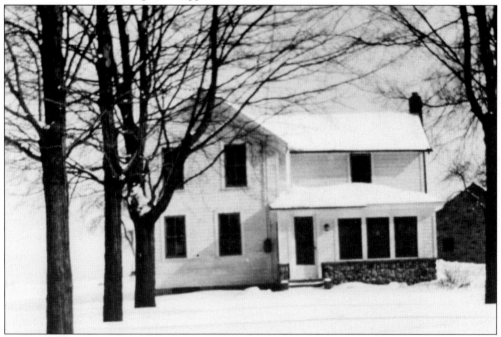

Northward on the east side of Lake Road was the Morehouse homestead. Joseph Morehouse and his brother-in-law, Nathan Raymond, settled here *c.* 1775. Women and children hid in a thicket on Morehouse Creek when the Mohawks came near. The house was demolished in 1995.

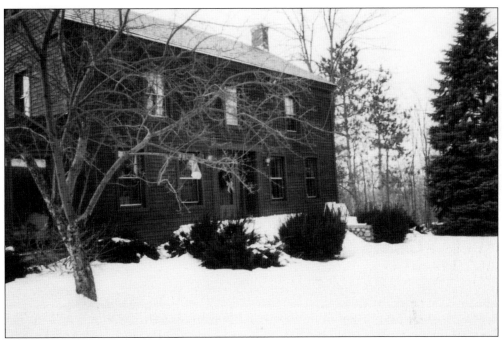

Zacheus Scribner built this house in 1773. He was one of the first members of Reverend Ball's church. Two of his sons, Aaron and Thaddeus, served in the militia. They asserted that they witnessed the surrender of Burgoyne in 1777. Thaddeus became Ballston's post rider. A honk from his horn meant a person had a letter. The residence is at 40 Lake Road.

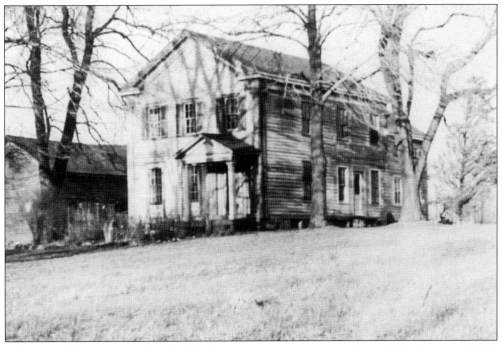

George Washington Beers etched his name on an upstairs window of this house in 1798. Community square dances were held here at 71 Lake Road.

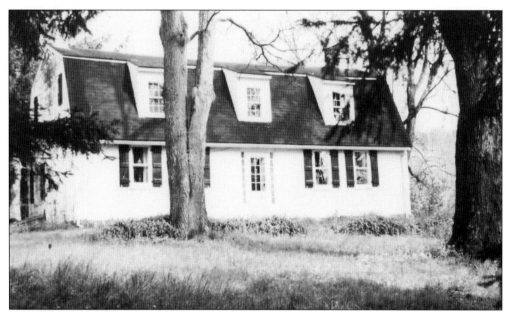

A diary was found in a closet in this house at 105 Lake Road. It was written in 1772 and described how a band of Indian warriors had camped between the house and the lake; they had captured two sons and a daughter and had taken them to a rock 1/2 mile from the house (possibly at the site of what is now known as Indian Rock). The daughter was scalped and killed.

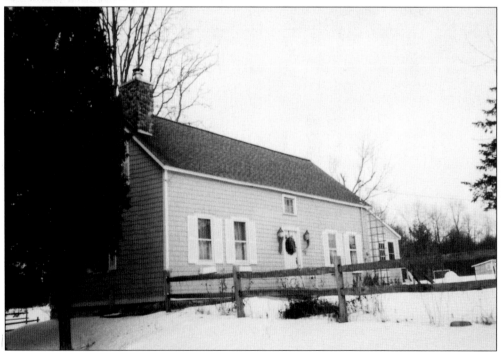

This early Dutch-style house is located at 139 Lake Road. Artifacts, such as creamware pottery, square nails, and panels painted Prussian blue and Venetian red, date the house to the late 1700s. A newspaper found plastered on a wall in the living room is dated 1793.

This stairway in the house at 139 Lake Road has had the treads turned over. One tread was a drawer in a chest! The original banister remains.

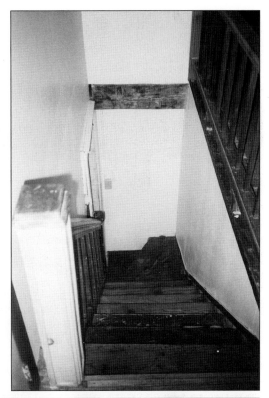

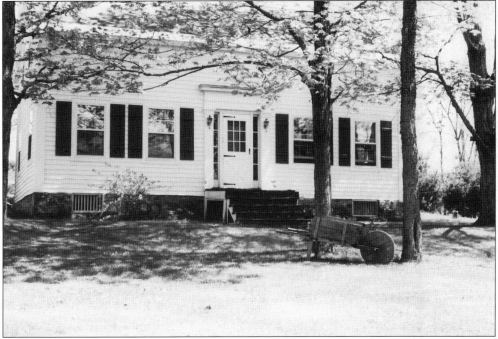

1848 is the year etched in the foundation of this house, located at 153 Lake Road. William Collamer wrote his name on the parlor room wall, and he is believed to be the builder. The Leahey family were later owners.

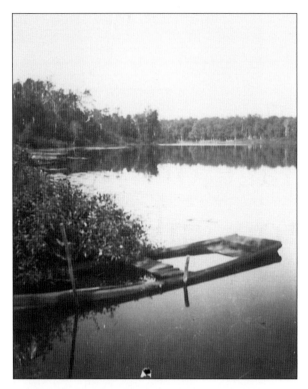

This photograph was taken on the northeast bank of Ballston Lake, facing south. The view is much like that seen by the Mohawks. One tale says that they visited an early settler and asked for cider. Since the cider had turned hard, the settler did not want to give them any; he told the the group to bring a basket the next day and he would fill it. The tribesmen returned with a willow basket that had been dipped in the lake and allowed to freeze, making a solid basket—they got their cider.

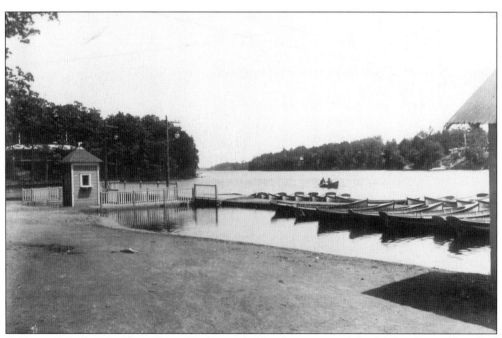

Canoes await the crowds at Forest Park, much like the canoes of the Mohawks two hundred years before.

Three
Village of
Ballston Lake

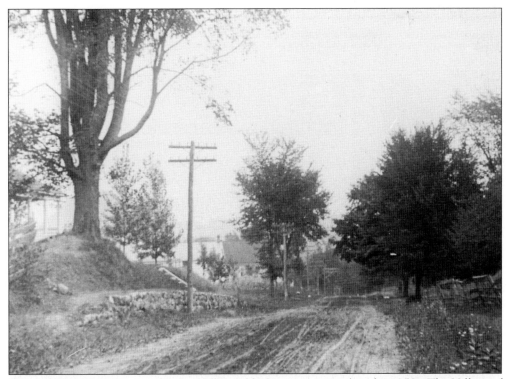

This is a view looking east on Lake Hill Road before it was paved in the 1950s. The Village of Ballston Lake was previously known as South Ballston and also the Branch, a name derived from the railroad crossings.

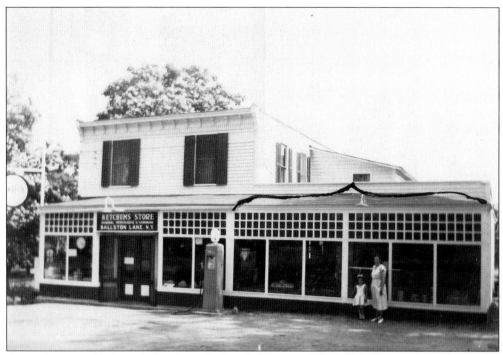

At the bottom of Lake Hill Road is a landmark known as Ketchum's Store. The structure was originally built by Mr. Mott, who opened it as a grocery store in the late 1800s. In 1926 John Ketchum converted it into a hardware store. Here, Lorene Ketchum, wife of Herb Ketchum, stands in front with her daughter, Muriel. At least four automobiles have gone through the front windows!

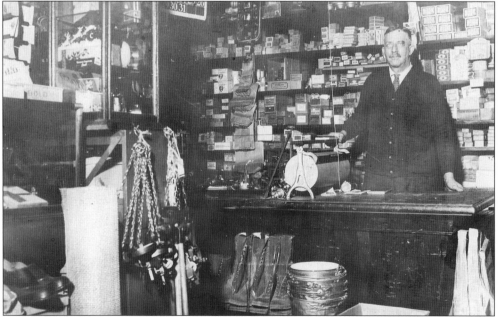

In this 1935 image, John M. Ketchum tends to his store, where he sold shovels for 95¢ and 5-gallon milk cans for $1.55.

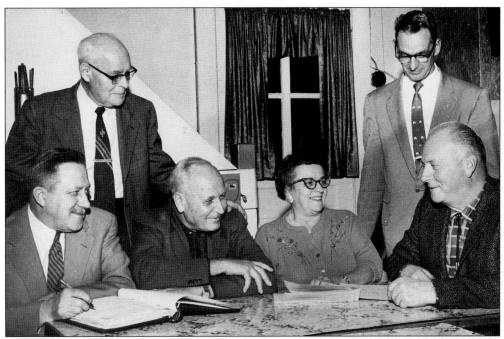

Ballston's Town Board met at members' houses. This picture was taken about 1960. From left to right are: Town Clerk Herb Ketchum, Judge John LeBast, Supervisor Alex Stewart, Highway Superintendent Ellen Winters, Councilman George Cole, and Judge Ernie Philips. Herb was the town clerk from 1941 to 1972, and never missed a meeting.

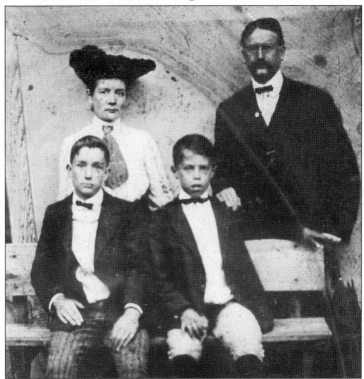

In 1899 President Theodore Roosevelt and his family visited Ballston Lake. In fact, his daughter, Alice, fell into a watering trough on Midline Road! This picture was taken in front of Ketchum's Store.

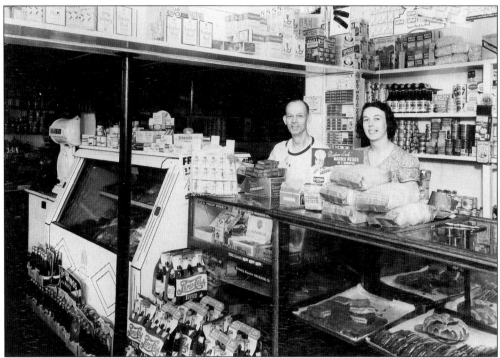

Located south on Main Street was Markham's Store. Charlie Markham and his daughter, Mary Elizabeth, are pictured in this 1937 photograph.

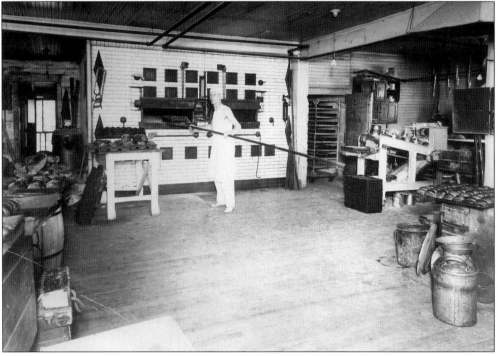

Charlie Markham operated a bakery with a room-sized oven. Many people remember that the bakery was always "a warm place that smelled so good."

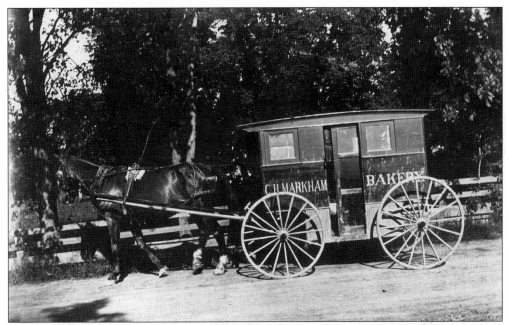

Markham's Bakery delivered to homes. Old Joe, the horse, was a faithful companion. The delivery route was 30 miles in length.

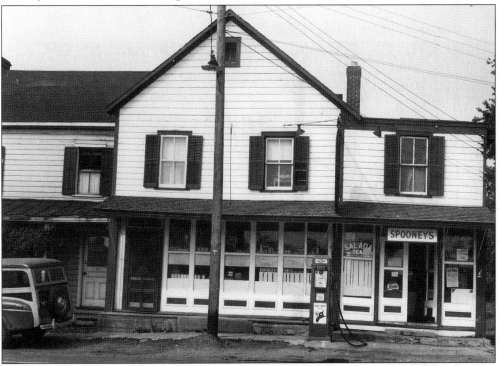

Harold Spoonogle purchased Markham's Store in 1944, and then John and Florence Fanning operated the store. It was destroyed by fire in 1962. Fanning's market was built farther west of the road and was owned by Ray and Connie Callanan since 1971. Fanning's was a town gathering place. It closed in 1997.

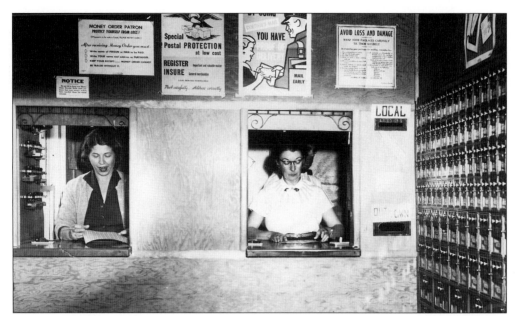

Ballston Lake's post office was in Markham's Store. Betty Spoonogle (left) and Gertrude Murnane (right) were postal clerks.

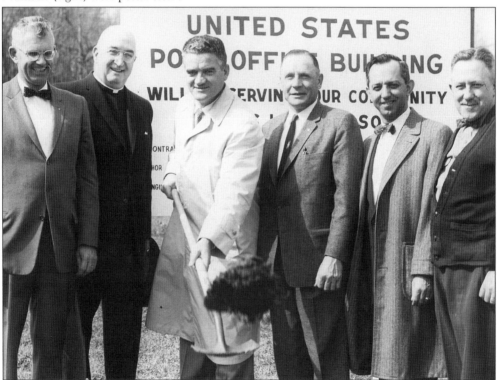

In 1960 a new Ballston Lake post office was built on Midline Road. Pictured at the ground breaking ceremony, from left to right, are: Postmaster Kenneth Smith, Rev. Leon Cartmell, William Egan, Clarence Beck, Nicholas Monsille, and Herbert Ketchum. This post office closed in 1996, when it was consolidated with Burnt Hills.

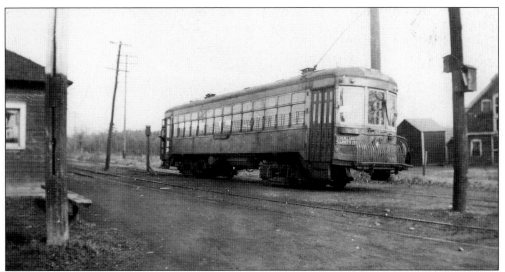

The trolley station was across Main Street from Fanning's market. The trolley was run by the Schenectady Railway Company from 1902 to 1941, and ran from Schenectady to Ballston Spa. A trip from Schenectady to Ballston Lake was 25¢, round trip.

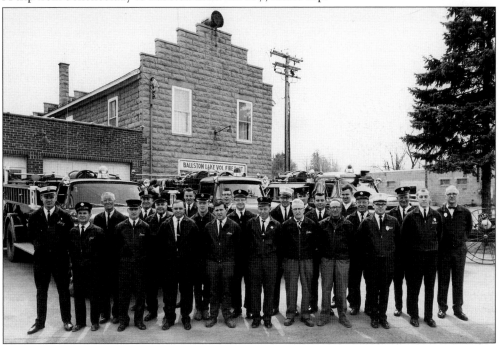

The Ballston Lake Volunteer Fire Department is an integral part of the community. In 1926 a second firehouse was built next to Markham's Store. This was fortunate for the Markham family, as the store burned several times. The firefighters of 1966 pose in front of the firehouse; they are, from left to right: (front row) Roy Justin, Joe Ross, Dave Lambert, Bill Hicks, Len Zullo, Charley Anderson, John Fanning, Lloyd Sauer, Bob McRoom, and Bill Gocha; (second row) Ted Gillingham, Bernard Tracey, Ken Wachtel, Werner Gibelius, Don Bennet, Bob Gocha, Vic Dussault, Earl Clogston, and Bill Ott; (third row) Wolf Schroeder, Art Swartz, Dennis Scales, John Mooney, and Walt Gillingham.

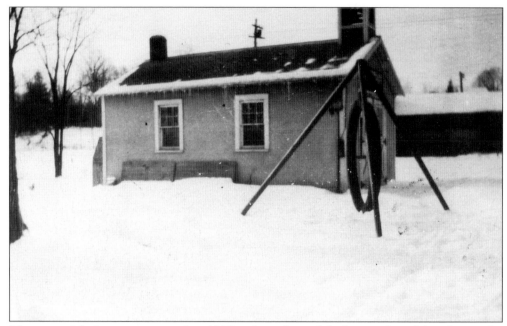

The original firehouse was erected in 1918 and was located farther south on Main Street. On Armistice Day, the townsfolk clanged the alarm and took out the firetruck to form a spontaneous parade. World War I was over!

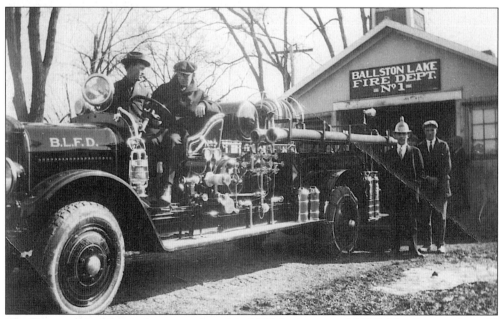

The first motorized firetruck was purchased in 1926 for just over $6,000. The Reo truck could seat two men.

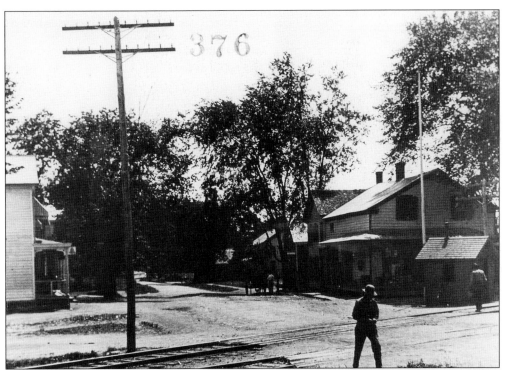

Frank Egan operated a grocery store on Main Street from 1879 until 1947. The D & H Railway station is shown here next to Egan's store. The station was a one-room hut that could accommodate five people. Joe Sarto, a Civil War veteran, was the flagman. Across the street at 17 Main Street was Egan's hotel. William Egan called his hotel Shen-andahora, meaning "near the beautiful water." Tom and Katherine McDonough ran Carney's, a tavern, for thirty-five years.

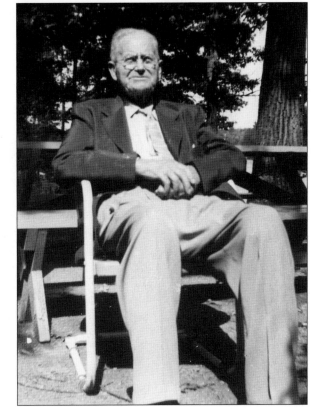

William Egan Sr. was the proprietor of the Ballston Lake hotel. He was the son of Patrick Egan, and William's wife was Mary Henessey.

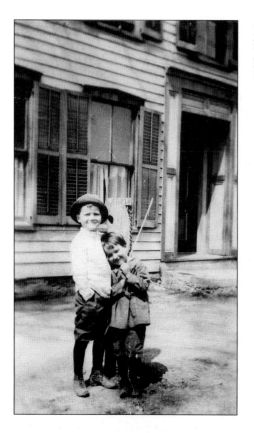

Bill Egan Jr. (left), age 6, is pictured here with his cousin Ed Kimball (right), age 4. The photograph was taken in 1920 on Main Street, Ballston Lake.

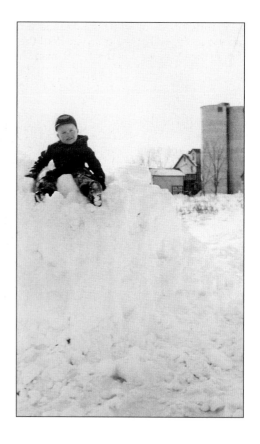

In this 1943 image, Richard Wagner sits on a snow bank. Parkis Mills can be seen in the background. The building was originally a cold storage facility for apples, which were shipped on trains. Henry Parkis converted the structure to a buckwheat and pancake mill. It was purchased in 1949 by the Tobin Packing Company.

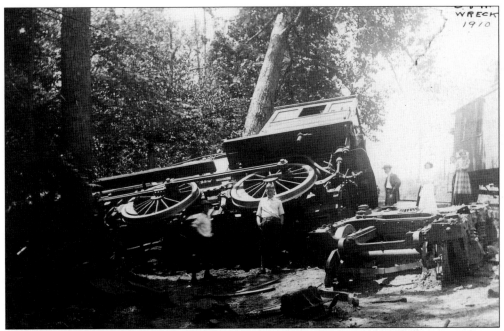

The railroad brought a business boom to Ballston. It was opened in 1831 and ran from Schenectady to Saratoga. Horses pulled the first cars and the trip took one hour. The Delaware and Hudson steam engines ran from 1877 until 1922. The steam engine announced its arrival in town with clouds of white smoke and a clanging bell. Children waved to the man in the caboose at the end of the train. In 1910 there was a D & H derailment along West Side Drive. During the Depression of the 1930s, many hobos rode the rails and begged food from townsfolk.

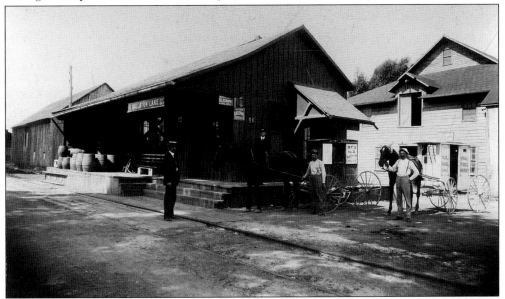

The railroad depot was next to the McKain Feed and Grain store. The telegraph was located at the depot, and mail was delivered by train three times a week. Pictured here, from left to right, in 1905 are station agent Hugh Davis; William Markham; and mail carriers Walter Osborne and Henry Merchant.

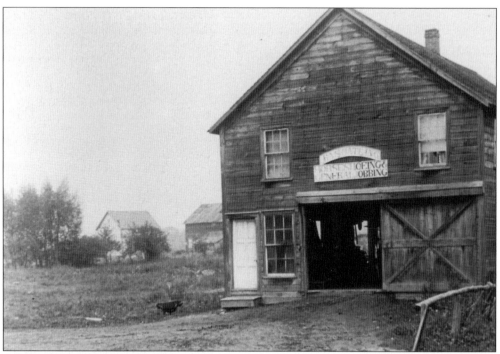

Bill Swatling and his sons, Lester and Steven, operated a blacksmith shop south on Main Street. Horses were shod here and iron shaped with forge and anvil.

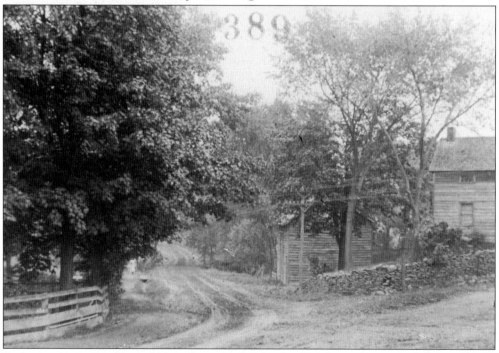

Today at the intersection of Main Street and Schauber Road stands a vintage house. It was owned by Jacob Boyce, who was a dealer in lumber and produce. The Clogston family later owned the house.

The Clogston brothers pose here in 1960. From left to right are: Earl, Jay, Roy, and Boyd Clogston. Jay and Earl were charter members of the Ballston Lake Volunteer Fire Department.

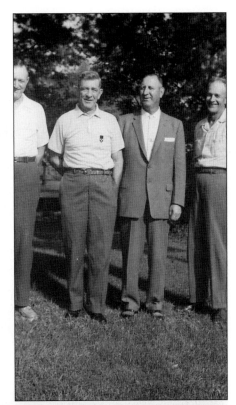

As with the Clogston family, other families remain an integral part of the community. Jane and Wendell Townley operated the Townley Funeral Home on Midline Road beginning in 1949. Wendell was president of the board of education and instrumental in forming the Ballston Lake Ambulance Squad.

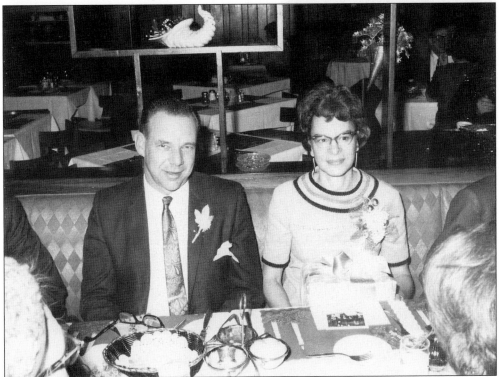

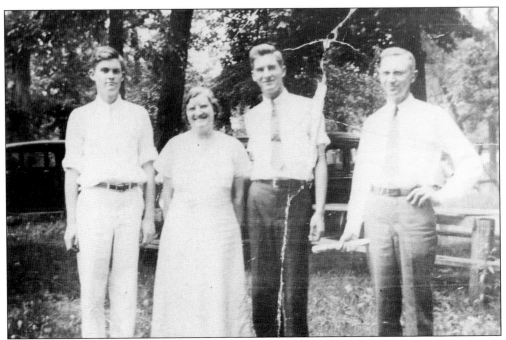

The Mengel family has long been active in Ballston. In 1931 they posed for a photograph; from left to right are: Jack, mother Maude, Art Jr., and father Arthur Mengel Sr. The Mengel Auditorium at the BH-BL High School is dedicated to Arthur Mengel Senior, who served on the board of education from 1932 to 1954.

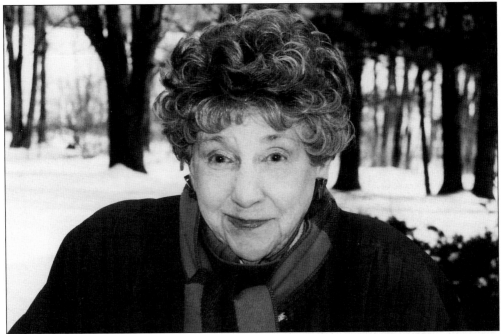

Lowanda Deegan of White's Beach Road was born in 1905. After twenty years of study, she graduated from the New York State University at Albany in 1996. Her major was English, and she was a favorite class member, as she baked cookies for the other students.

Florence and Carl Breitbeck pose here with their daughter, Sandy, in 1947. Florence is a direct descendent of John and Priscilla Alden of Mayflower fame. Florence was active as a Girl Scout leader, Carl worked for the *Schenectady Gazette* for forty years, and Sandy won awards in horsemanship.

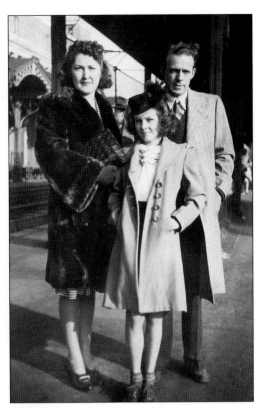

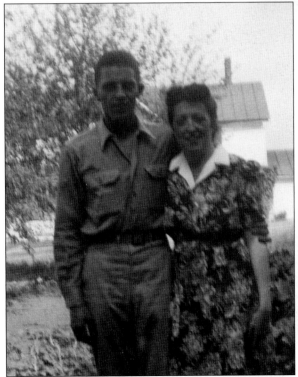

Bill and Mary Clancy Quellhorst lived on West Side Drive. Mary taught in the BH-BL school district for twenty years. Bill was a light machine gunner in the 29th Division. He was killed outside St. Lo, France, in 1944.

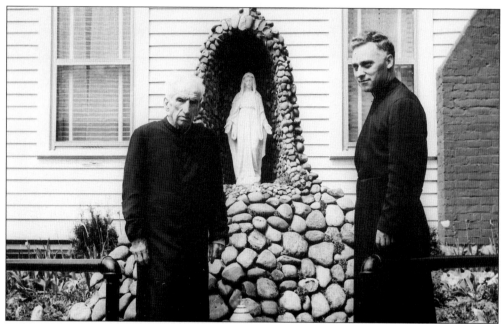

Father Daniel Hogan (left) was assigned to Our Lady of Grace parish in 1922. He would serve that church until his death in 1967. He was an accomplished athlete and friends with greats such as Jack Dempsey and Mike McTigue. Father Hogan organized a boys club and summer camp, where boxing was taught. He stands with Father Carr in front of the grotto by the old rectory on Edward Street. The grotto was built by a grateful student, John Mancini.

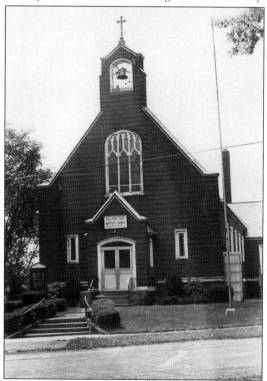

Our Lady of Grace Church on Edward Street was dedicated in 1924 and served the congregation until 1973, when the church moved to Midline Road. In the later 1940s, townsfolk flocked to the basement on Sunday nights to watch Milton Berle, as the church had one of the first televisions. The church is now the Ballston Lake Baptist Church.

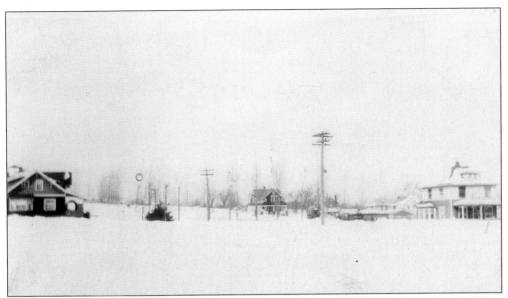

The housing development known as Buell Heights was built c. 1905 by the Moore family. They named the streets after their relatives: Buell Avenue for Samuel Buell; Charles Street for Charles Markham; Edward Street for Edward Moore; and William Street for William Tierney. This view is facing north on Buell Avenue, 12 Buell on the left, and 4 Edward on the right. Charles Street is in the background.

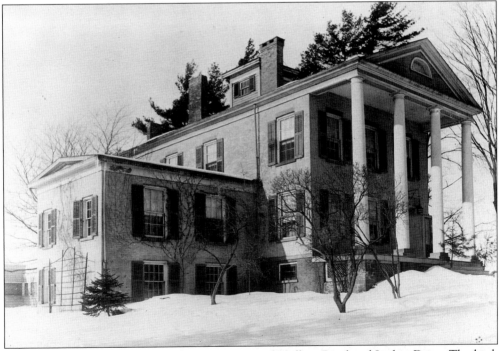

The Buell Mansion is located at the intersection of Midline Road and Larkin Drive. The back portion is believed to have been built by Beriah Palmer, a founding father of the town. The front portion was built by Reverend Edward Davis, the founder of the Calvary Episcopal Church. A Tory was once hanged near this house.

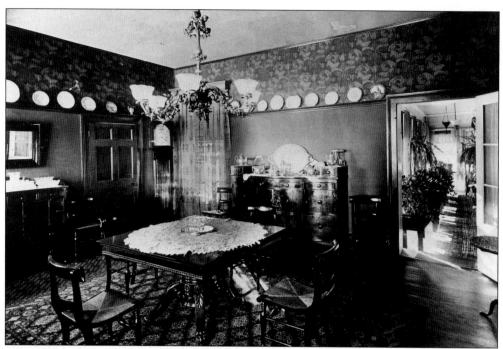

The elaborate dining room of the Buell Mansion depicts the vast wealth of the early owners. A dumbwaiter enabled the domestic servants to send food up from the kitchen. There is a curious trap door in the kitchen that leads to an underground tunnel to the barn.

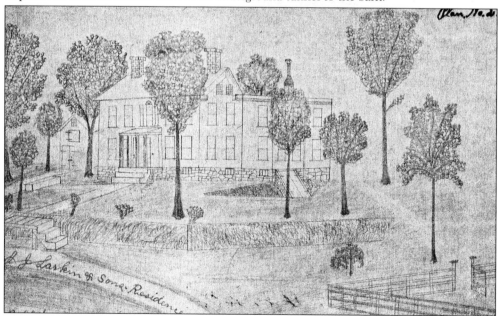

The Larkin house is located at 5 Larkin Drive, next to the Buell Mansion. The homestead dates back to the late 1700s. A large iron key still locks the ancient front door. The family tin lantern was kept by the front door. These lanterns held candles, and the tin had holes punched in it, making a decorative pattern. Each family had a different pattern so one would know who was approaching.

44

John Larkin married Loretta Delong in 1899. He was the son of Anson and Sybil Larkin. This is their wedding picture.

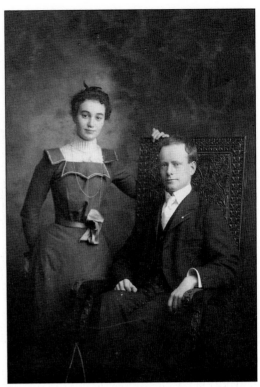

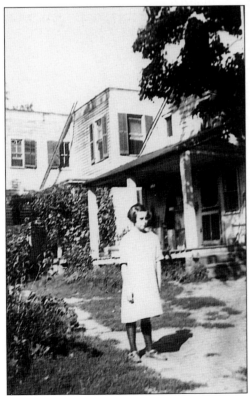

Mary Dunn in 1923 stands in the backyard of the Larkin home. She is the daughter of John and Loretta Larkin. Her sisters were named Etta and Sybil. Mary is a member of the first graduating class of the BH-BL High School.

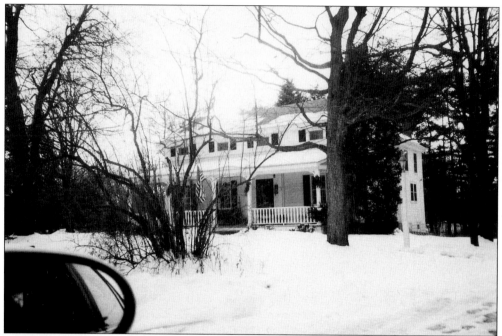

Peter Bliss and his wife, Ann Townley, were the parents of ten children. They lived in this house at 99 Midline while Peter worked as foreman of laborers of the Buell Mansion. A penny found in the fireplace mantel was minted in 1844.

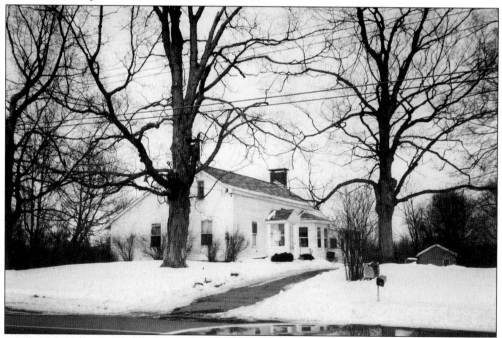

This early home, facing south, is at the intersection of Midline Road and Route 50. It was the homestead of Thomas and Jesse Smith. The brothers fought in the Revolution for the Americans. When they returned home, they found their cabin burned. They rebuilt with hewn green timber.

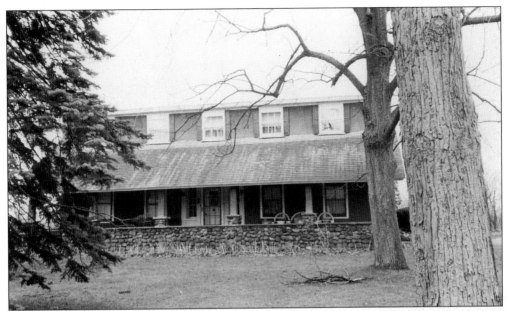

This inn and tavern at 924 Saratoga Road was originally owned by Joseph Bettys, the father of the infamous Tory spy, Joe Bettys. The spy was a Revolutionary War courier of messages from Canada to New York City. He was also responsible for the capture of Patriots from Ballston. Joe was captured and hanged in Albany on April Fool's Day, 1782. People lined the streets to witness the hanging "as if King George himself was passing by."

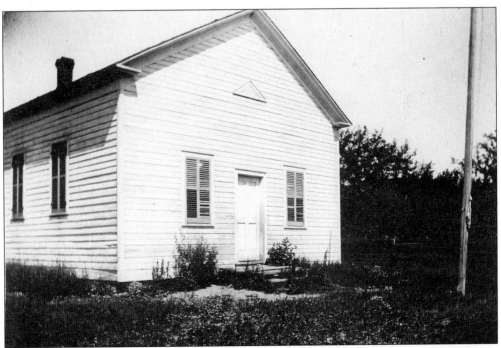

Continuing north on Route 50 was District School #11, on the west side of the road. It has been moved to the east side and is now a private residence. Students were taught "reading, writing, and 'rithmatic," and yes, they did walk 2 miles to school!

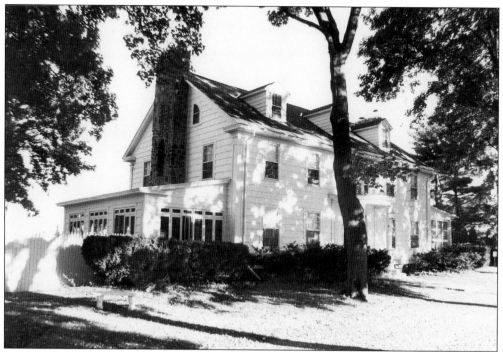

Lake Ridge Farm has a commanding view of Ballston Lake, and the mountains of Vermont can be seen on a clear day. Early owners include Calvin Calkins, Mr. Manning, J.B. White, and the Cappiellos.

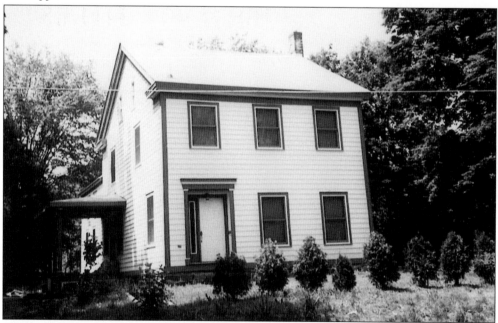

This early homestead is located at 1049 Saratoga Road. The original owner is unknown; however, there are indications that the structure dates to the late 1700s. Researching early deeds can be a complicated process because landmarks, such as "a heap of stones" and a tree marked with an "X," were often used.

Four

Burnt Hills

Burnt Hills was named from the Native American practice of burning the fields. The new growth after the fire would entice game for easy hunting. S & D Beers drew this 1866 map of the intersections of Kingsley Road (then North and South Streets) and Lake Hill Road (then East and West Streets).

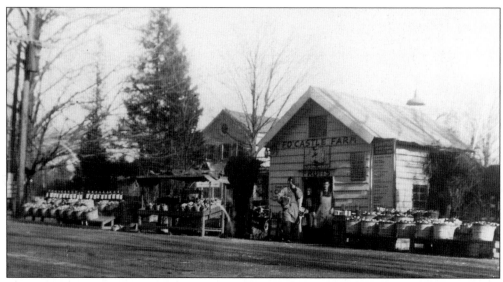

Fo'Castle Farm is located on the east side of Kingsley Road. It was opened in 1906 by Claude Bailey, and the store was named for the forecastle of a ship where the crew slept. Elmar, Dale, and Elwood Kline (from left to right) stand in front of the store in this 1937 photograph. The store is now owned by Alan and Caran Collyer.

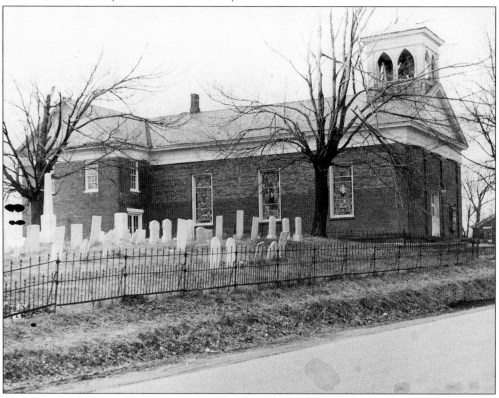

The Burnt Hills Baptist Church was organized in 1783, and the brick church was built in 1839. The adjacent Hillside Cemetery is the resting place of founding families such as Kingsley, Waterman, Hollister, Schauber, and Larkin.

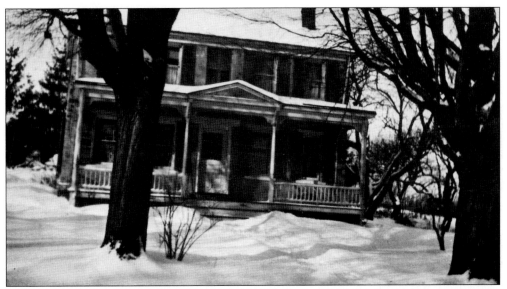

Abigail Cunningham leased this house from Abel Minard in 1857. It is located just north of the Baptist church. She lived here with her daughter, Eliza, until her death in 1890. Leon and Norma Turpit purchased the home in 1925.

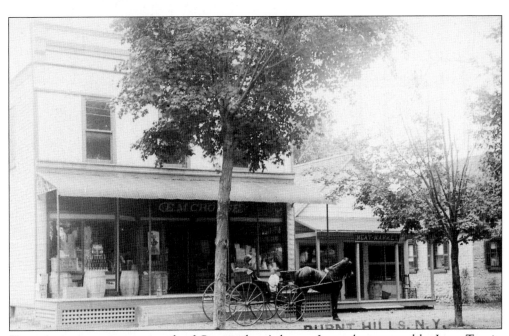

Crouse's grocery store was north of Cunningham's house. It was later owned by Leon Turpit. Henry Sharpley operated a meat market next door. Bands of gypsies raided the markets and pick-pocketed the goods.

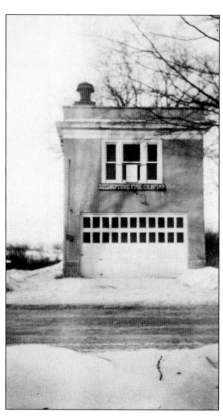

The Burnt Hills Neptune Volunteer Fire Department was formed in 1918. The company's first pumper was financed by Earl Townley and Gilbert Seelye. It was stored in a firehouse built by the firemen.

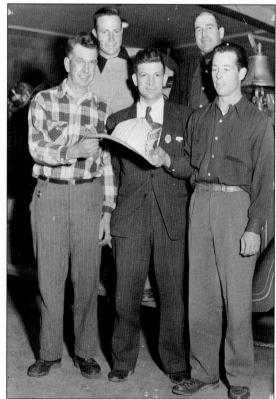

Firemen pose here in this 1948 photograph. Pictured, from left to right, are Gordy Sack, Jack Wolfe, and Howard Plummer in front. Kim Sack (left) and Len Palmatier stand in back.

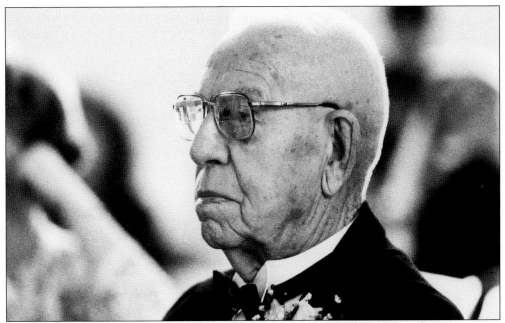

Earl and Nora Smith lived across the street from the fire department and ran a grocery store. Earl (shown here) was a charter member of the BH-BL Rotary Club and served as historian of that organization. Other charter members were: Raymond Ashdown, Stanley Ashdown, George Bailey, George Bates, Charles Cruikshank, Ross Cunningham, Willard Dyer, Axel Freiberg, Stanley Garrison, John Heckler, Charles Kaulfuss, Stanley Knight, Donald MacElroy, John MacElroy, Elmer MacArthur, Lester McCormack, Albert Merchant, Stephen Merchant, Frank Mooney, Ralph Palmer, Donald Potter, I. Ben Rubin, Gilbert Seelye, J. Donald Scott, Daniel Smith, Elmer Smith, Henry Solomon, Francis Stevens, Alex Stewart, Clement Tomlins, John Tillburg, Harmon Wade, Frederick Waldbillig, and Arthur Young. The club received its charter in 1951.

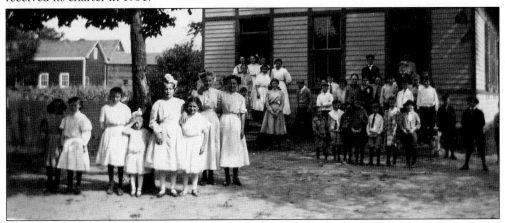

A two-room school was once located at the intersection of Kingsley and Lake Hill Roads. The front room was for grades 5–8, and the back was for grades 1–5. Children attended school in the winter and the summer, as they were needed at home during spring planting and fall harvesting. Mary Streever, Pearl Bubb, and Eva Holbrook were teachers. John Marvin was a teacher from New York City; he was later thrown out the school window by the students and never came back!

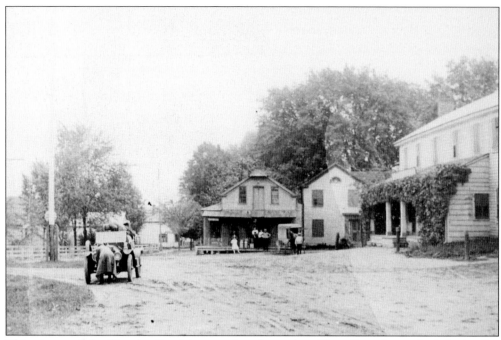

This picture of the Kingsley Road intersection shows the village flagpole on the left; the flag was raised and lowered each day. Walter Johnson ran a grocery store here that dates to the early 1800s. Tales were swapped around the potbelly stove and contests were held as to who could eat the most bananas. The store was also used as a polling place and post office. The Kingsley Inn is on the right; the inn was opened *c.* 1795 by William Kingsley and was a stop on the stagecoach route from Schenectady to Ballston Spa. The inn had twenty-five rooms, wide plank flooring, and a huge pine bar.

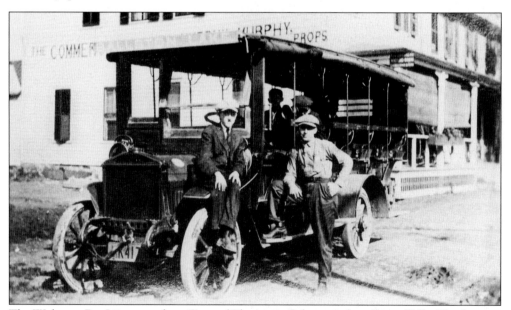

The Welcome Bus Line went from General Electric in Schenectady to Burnt Hills. This bus was called the Irish Kate. Travel became easier when some roads were paved in the 1920s.

This house at 101 Lake Hill Road was owned by Cady Hollister, J. Mott, and N. Seelye. It was originally built in 1796 as a frame cottage. The front portion was added about 1810. The center hall stairway railing has been polished by generations of hands sliding up and down. Connie and Harold Falconer purchased the house in 1936.

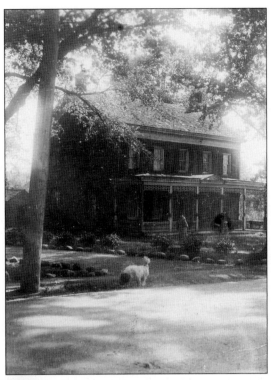

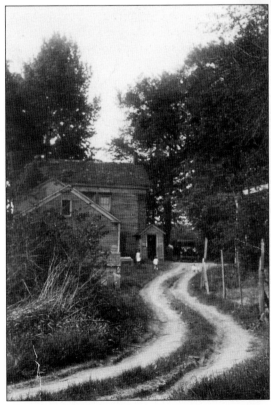

The back of the Falconer farm had an apple orchard that covered 12 acres. Connie Falconer recalled, "The orchard was planted with a spade in one hand and a Cornell bulletin in the other." Cherries, peaches, plums, and pears were grown as well.

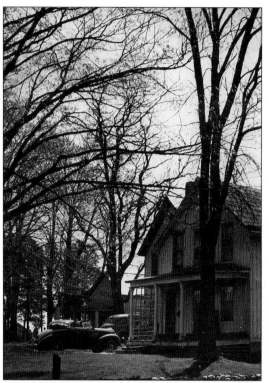

This house at 87 Lake Hill Road was built by Isaac Sears. It was owned by James Wilson Abbs. He married Maggie Warner. Their daughter, Mary Abbs, was called the belle of Burnt Hills because of her beauty and popularity.

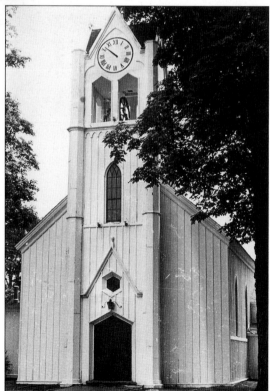

The first service held at the Calvary Episcopal Church was on Christmas, 1849. Reverend Edward Davis was the first rector. Several Civil War veterans are buried in the adjoining cemetery.

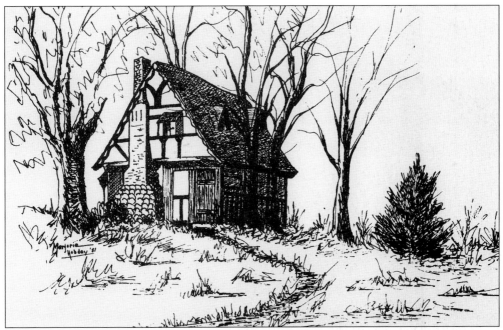

Farther east on the north side of Lake Hill Road, George Shorey built his artist studio about 1914. He taught art classes here during the summer season. This pen and ink drawing of the studio was done by Majorie Hobday.

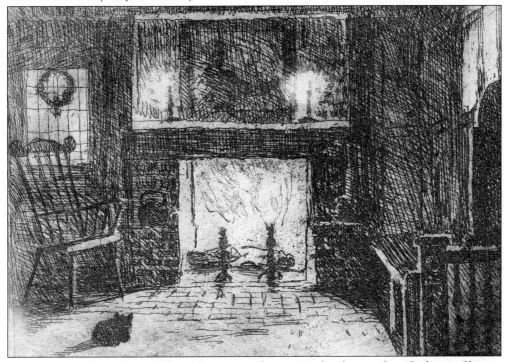

The interior of the studio was drawn by George Shorey. His daughter-in-law, Catherine Shorey, lives in the house west of the studio. The house was built in 1793 and has been in the Jones/Shorey family for generations.

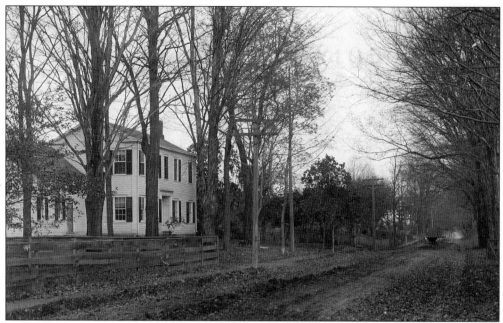

The Townley house on Lake Hill Road was the home of Earl and Jessie Townley. They moved there in 1920. Earl was an insurance and real estate agent. Jessie ran a tearoom at her home, called the Holly Hock Tea Shop.

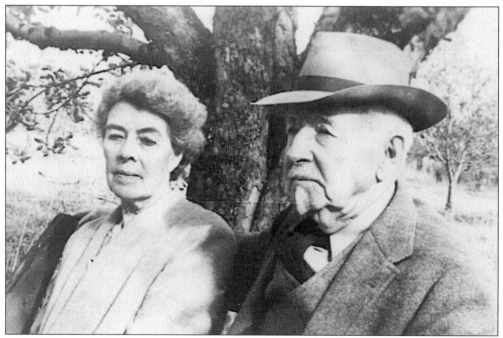

Commander Claude Bailey and his wife, Emily Moore, are pictured here. They were married in 1900. The commander was an influential member of the committee to consolidate the one-room schoolhouses. The couple retired to "Three Acres" in 1944.

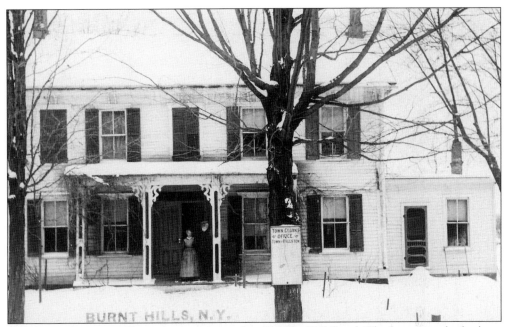

This house, known as Three Acres, is located at 82 Lake Hill Road. The house was built about 1830 and was also known as the Pink House, after Jacob and Jessie Pink, who lived there for years. The residence was the town clerk's office when Charles Upham lived there. Many marriage licenses were issued from the house. Commander Bailey laid the hearthstone, which came from his boyhood home in Arkansas, here at his retirement home.

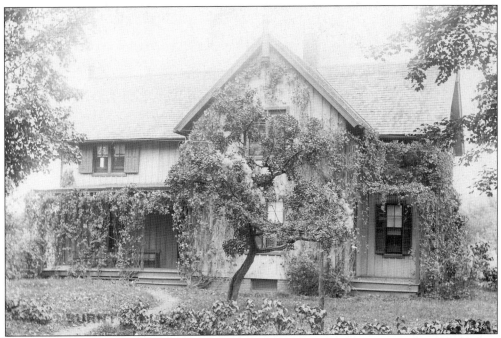

Next to Three Acres is the parsonage of the Calvary Episcopal Church. It was purchased by Dr. Edward Davis and has housed rectors since the 1850s.

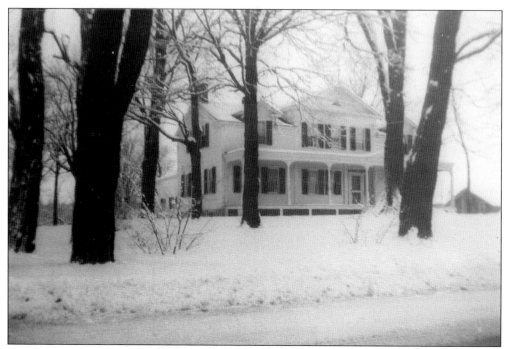

The Gilbert Seelye house at 96 Lake Hill Road originally faced east. The newel post contains a silver quarter minted in 1825. Gilbert Seelye served as a state senator for twenty-two years, from 1939 to 1960.

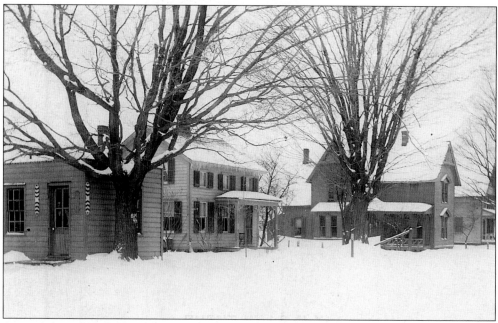

Around the corner on Kingsley Road and to the north was Bayliss' barber shop and the Dave Bayliss home. The barber shop was a small red frame building. Each patron had his own shaving mug with his initials on it. A shave cost 10¢ and a hair-cut cost two bits. This was a gathering place for games and gossip.

Farther north lived Valentine Bubb and his wife, Pearl Larkin. They were married in 1915 and were the parents of Bernice Knight. Valentine made milk deliveries, worked for General Electric, and served as Burnt Hills postmaster. He was a charter member of the Burnt Hills fire company.

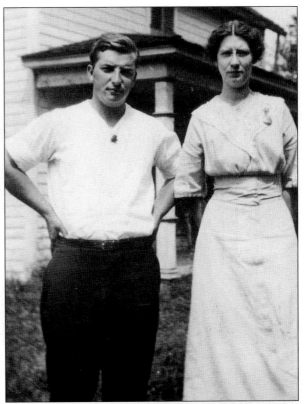

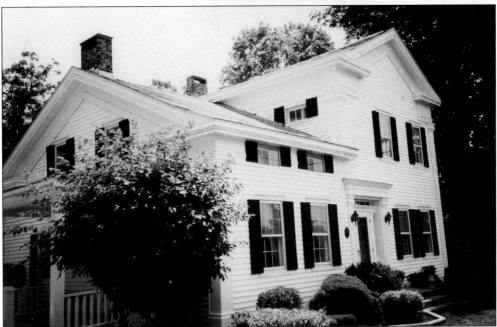

Asa Waterman settled farther north at 850 Saratoga Road. He, like so many Revolutionary pensioners, claimed he carried Benedict Arnold from the battlefield at Bemis Heights in 1777 and later regretted the deed when Arnold was found to be a traitor.

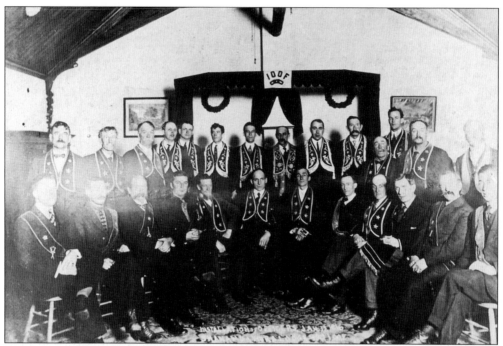

On the north side of Lake Hill Road, going west, was the Shanendahora Lodge #499 of the Odd Fellows. The club was organized in 1889 and initially met at the Buell Mansion. They moved to Burnt Hills *c.* 1904. The building was destroyed by fire in 1917. Early members included Charles Markham, Ira Abbs, Valentine Bubb, Leon Turpit, and David Waite.

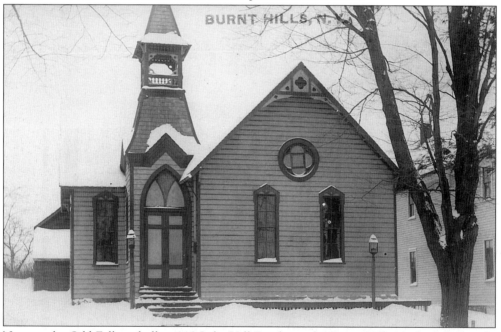

Next to the Odd Fellows hall at 110 Lake Hill Road was the Burnt Hills Methodist Church. The original church was built in 1874 and served twenty-five families. The Methodist church congregation moved to its present location north of this building in 1954.

In this photograph, chickens peck at the intersection of Lake Hill Road and Route 50! The latter was known as "convict road," as it was built in the early 1920s, and prisoners had constructed it. The Witbeck house is shown on the right, at 120 Lake Hill Road.

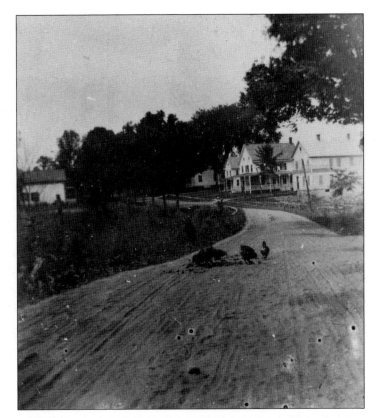

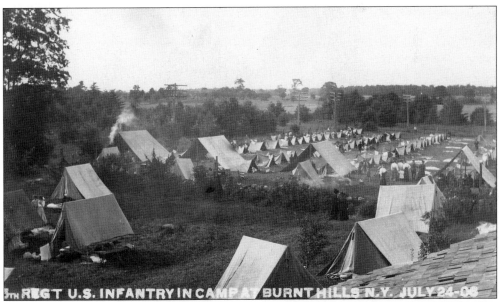

5TH REGT U.S. INFANTRY IN CAMP AT BURNT HILLS N.Y. JULY 24-06

In 1906 the United States Infantry 5th Regiment encamped on fields in Burnt Hills. The soldiers were marching south from Plattsburg.

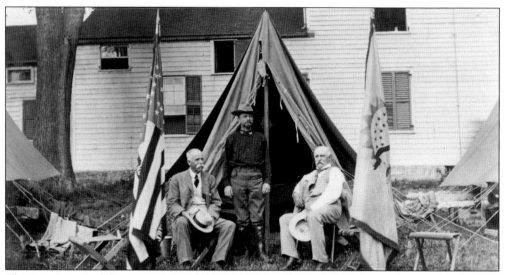

This is a picture of the command tent of Colonel Cowles on Lakeville Road.

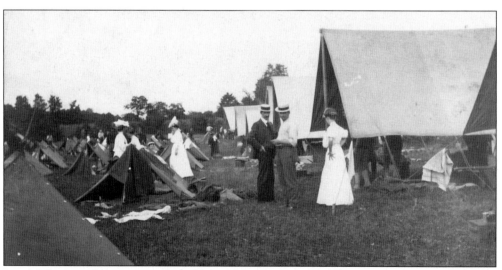

Local folks turned out to meet the soldiers at the encampment.

Five

BH-BL School

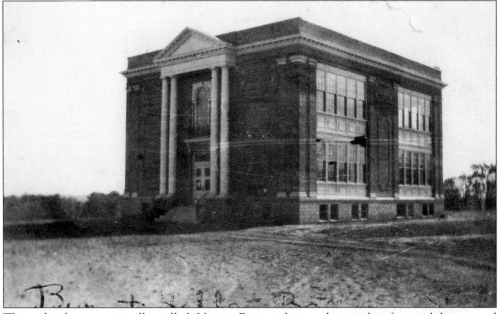

This school was originally called Union Free and was the result of consolidation and centralization of several one-room schoolhouses. It was opened in the fall of 1916 for forty-eight students. It burned in 1929 and was then rebuilt and expanded. The yearbook was entitled *The Hilltop*. After a location for the school was determined, Claude Bailey and George Schauber moved the location stake southward, some 50 feet, providing the spacious lawn in front of the school.

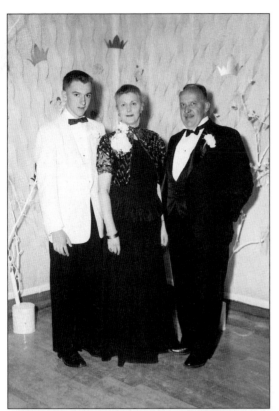

The school, now known as Stevens Elementary School, is named for Francis Stevens, who came to the school as a teacher in 1928. He served until 1967. He married Mabel Aldrich. They are shown with their son, Bud.

The graduating class of 1929 included, from left to right: (front row) Anita Egan, Lucy Zani, Francis Lamoreaux, Martha Plummer, Isabel Hewitt, Barbara Marvin, and Frances Moore; (back row) Harry Dalbey, William Davis, Viola Van Patten, Marguerite Willis, Louis Lafforthun, and Louis Baumgartner.

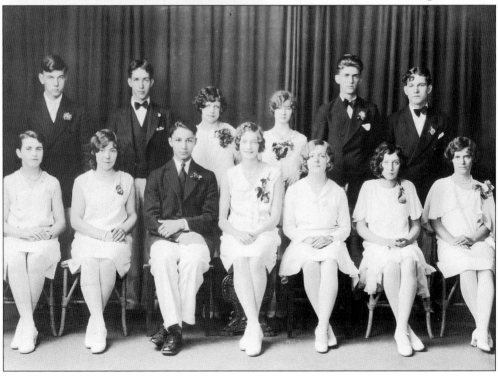

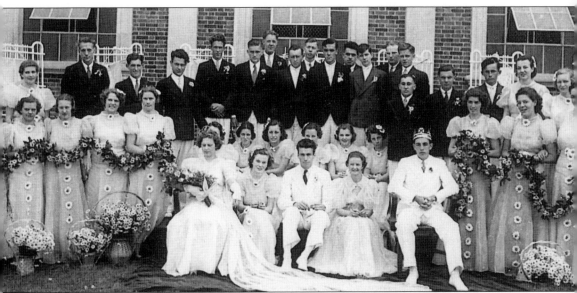

Class Day was held on May 1, 1937. A king and queen were chosen, and students danced around a Maypole. From left to right are: (front row) Myrna Van Patten, Virginia Donley, John Sarto, Evelyn Casey, and Stanley Garrison; (second row, standing) Doris Collins, Ruth Hammond, Lucy Murray, Virginia Fox, and Isabelle Fobian; (second row, seated) Minnie Boswell, Beverly Williams, Eleanor Brust, Louise Strelow, Barbara Piercy, and Margaret Dole; (standing, right) Helen Piercy, Dorothy Kolor, and Loretta Curran; (back row, standing) Elizabeth Hammond, Emil Donald Flicker, Walter Morris, Arthur Curtis, Lloyd Taylor, Louis Sammler, Norman Lamb, Vernon Van Patten, Donald Waite, Melvin Smith, Stanley Liebert, Robert Kimball, Wright Aldridge, Fred Foss, Robert LeMay, Andrew Caldwell, Marvin Arnold, Eleanor Deland, and Elizabeth Jackson.

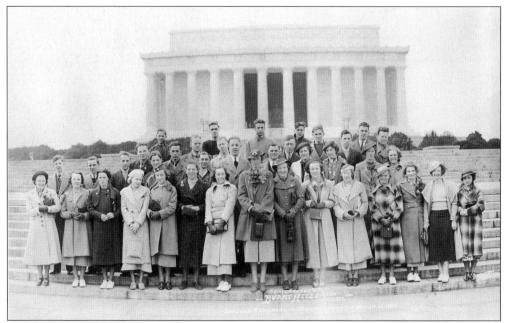

The Class of 1937 are pictured here during their visit to Washington, D.C. The trip was an annual event for each graduating class.

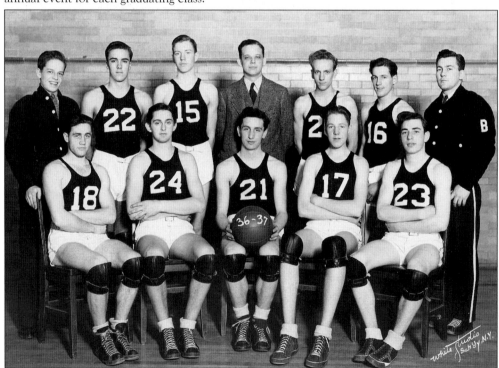

Pictured here is the boys' basketball team of 1936–37. Seated, from left to right, are: Sam Benjamen, Jim Yates, Louis Eager, Norman Lamb, and Stan Garrison; standing, from left to right, are: Fred Foss, Melvin Smith, Donald Waite, Fred Crum, Don Flicker, Walter Morris and coach Ray Benjamen.

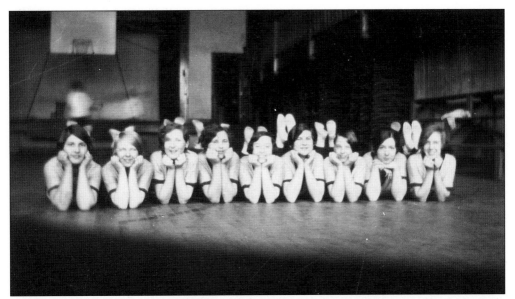

Pictured here is the girls' basketball team of 1928. From left to right are: Elizabeth Peck, Lorraine Raino, Dorothy Johnson, Anita Egan, Sybil Larkin, Dorothy Egan, Mary Schauber, Marion Hewitt, and Elizabeth Jackson. The coach was Trudi Rice.

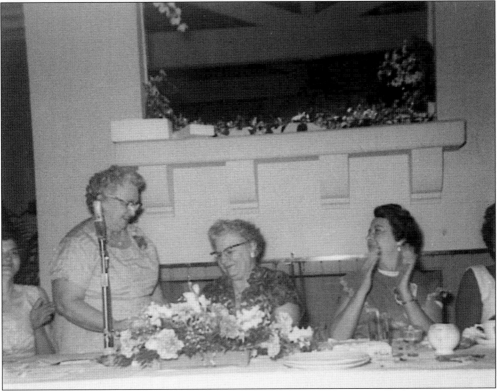

Miss Trudi Rice (center) was honored by Margaret Mooney (left) and Anita Wagner (right). Miss Rice organized the Women's Recreation class in 1925 and also taught fourth grade for many years.

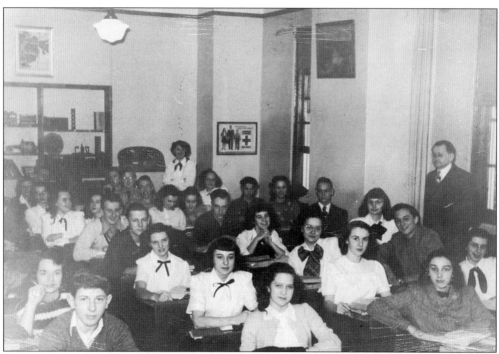

Charles Wilde taught this English class in 1948. Seated directly in front of him are, from left to right, Mary Rose, Ken Tibbits, and Bev Stephenson.

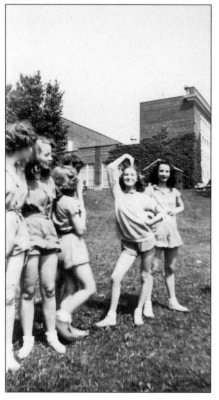

These girls are gym class cut-ups, *c.* 1947–48. From left to right are: Karolyn Bardin, Marjorie Hobday, Virginia Bigwood, unidentified, Evelyn Dadez, and Katherine Jones.

Six
Middle Line Road

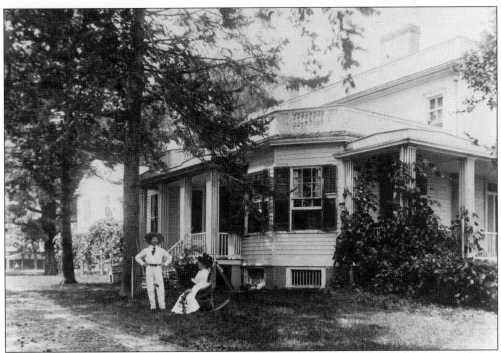

Middle Line Road was named because it was the middle of the 5-mile square when the township was surveyed. "Hawkwood" was located on the west side of Middle Line Road, north of Route 50. Captain Guy Baker and his wife Countess Dicisonia pose in this 1880 photograph. The house was first built *c*. 1790. Henry Walton, Esq., lived there, followed by Edward Delevan. The home contained four pianos, eleven fireplaces, European art treasures, and the first gas lights in town. Unfortunately, all that remains today is a collapsed windmill and open wells because a fire destroyed the mansion in 1965.

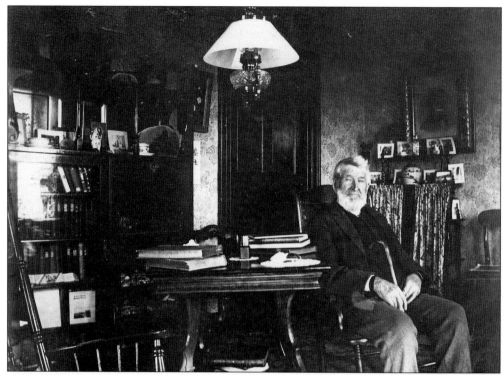

Thomas Feeney bought the land adjacent to Hawkwood on the north side about 1830. Thomas was born in Ireland and his wife-to-be, Mary Carter, was born in Scotland. They immigrated to the United States on the same boat! Thomas was a foreman at Hawkwood and was the father of six boys and six girls.

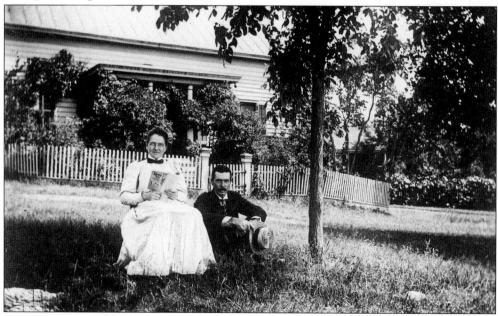

Emma, daughter of Thomas Feeney, poses with husband, Miles Betts, in front of the Feeney house. The house was torn down in 1910. The fourth generation of Feeneys reside on the land.

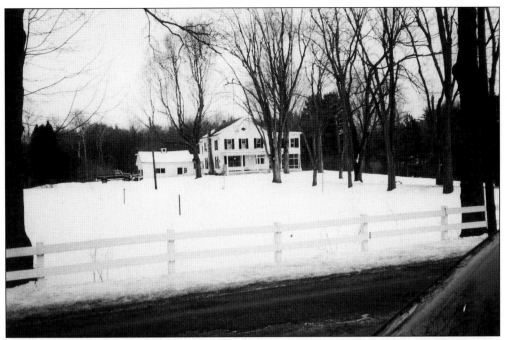

Across the street from Hawkwood is a home lived in by A.W. Curtiss. It was later owned by the Neddleton family.

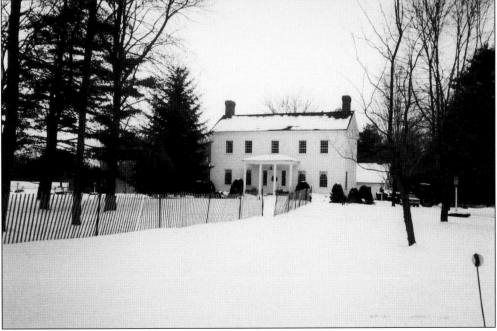

The front door windows and stairway are original to this house that has been moved from Middle Line Road to "the Lane." The Lane, also known as Lovers' Lane, connects Middle Line Road to Goode Street. Hezekiah Middlebrook lived in the house. He was a founding member of Eliphalet Ball's church. Hezekiah claimed that he ran into Joe Bettys just before the invasion of 1780. Joe warned him of the incoming invasion and then disappeared into the brush.

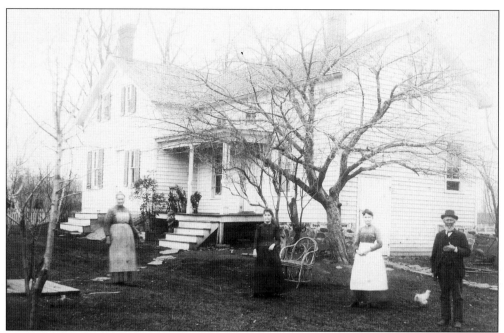

This house at 76 Middle Line Road was originally owned by Elizabeth and Asa Hollister. Later, the Simeon Davis family lived here. Mother Laura (far left) and daughters Emma (center) and Sophrona (right), are pictured with father Simeon. Sisters Emma and Satie quarreled, and although they lived in the same house, they did not speak to each other for years. They even maintained separate gardens and did their canning individually.

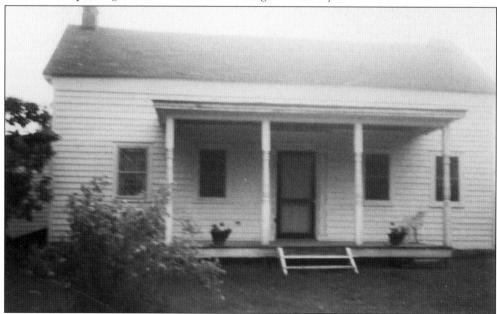

This house at 79 Middle Line Road was once the Ballston Center Post Office. It was established in the early 1800s. Mail was delivered by stage or horseback. Samuel Cook was an early postmaster. Postage to congressmen was free, and Samuel Cook promised free postage for the Ballston Center Presbyterian Church while he was postmaster.

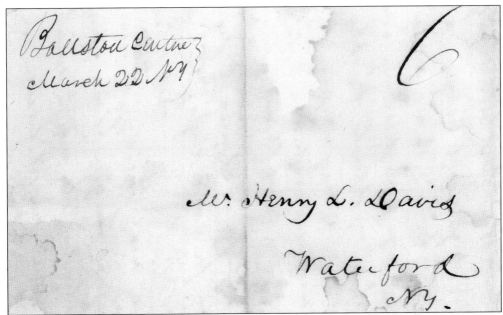

This letter was mailed from the Ballston Center Post Office in 1837. It was from Edward Davis to his cousin, Henry Davis. It is an example of a stampless cover. No envelopes were used, and the postmaster handwrote the cost of postage, which was determined by how far the letter was going.

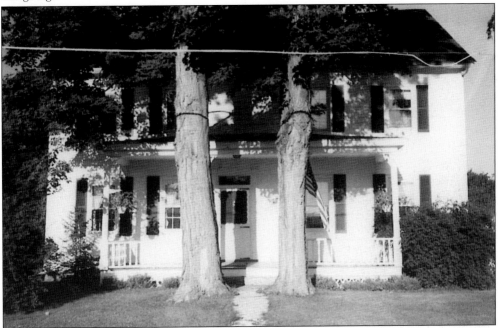

Samuel Southard operated a tavern at the intersection of Middle Line Road and Charlton Road. The building dates to about 1807. Tavern patrons were told to watch "their p's and q's," which stood for pints and quarts. Bar bills were kept on a blackboard. The tavern owner did not hold the Presbyterian church in high regard. Once, during a wind storm, part of the steeple was blown over. He gleefully announced to his customers that "the devil had lost its tail."

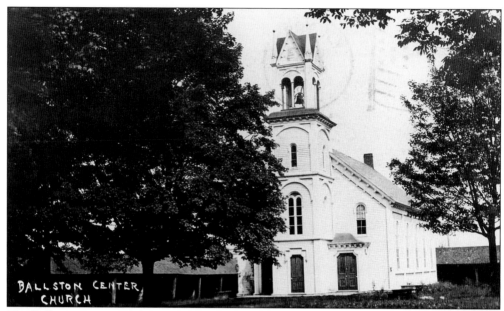

The Ballston Center Presbyterian Church was founded in 1775 by Reverend Eliphalet Ball. It was moved to the corner of Charlton and Middle Line Road in 1803. This 1908 photograph shows horse sheds on the west and north sides of the building. The church burned in 1993 and was rebuilt.

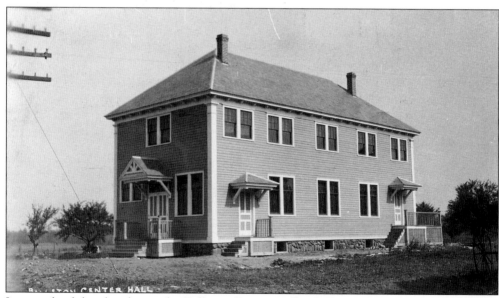

Just north of the church was the Ballston Grange Hall, which was built in 1910. It was the social center of Ballston Center. The building was demolished in 1992.

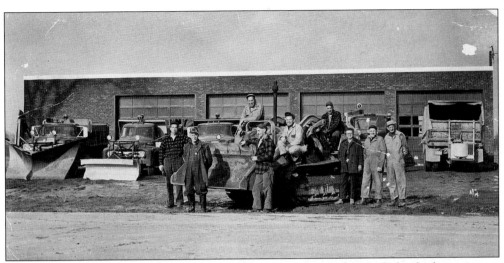

The Town of Ballston Highway Department pose here in front of the highway garage on Charlton Road in 1959. From left to right are: Don Marks, Bill Bliss, Al Merchant, Jim Werner, Frank Van Vorst, Howard Plummer, Superintendent Ellen Winters, Wesley Sherwood and Bill Trieble.

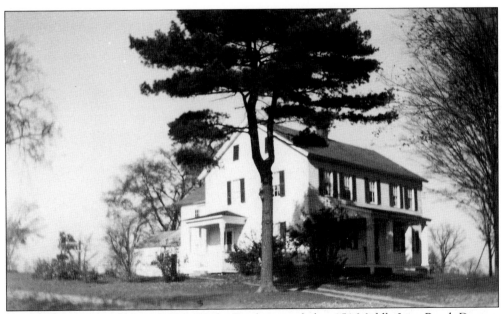

Dr. Samuel Davis and his wife Mary Kirby Dunham settled at 151 Middle Line Road. Doctors studied for two years in order to get their medical degree. "Aunt Jenny" was the Davis children's nanny. She warned them not to go swimming in Ballston Lake because of the panthers and wolves in the area. The house is believed to be a stop (or hold) on the Underground Railroad. In 1942 Ruth and Glen Center bought the house, and while renovating, they found a secret room behind the staircase.

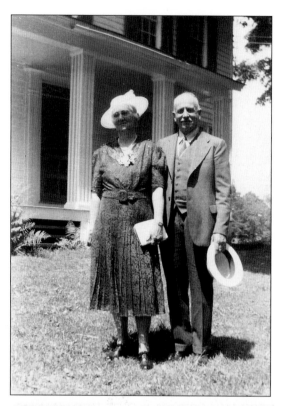

Stephen Henry Merchant and his wife Alice Morehouse stand in front of the Centers' home in 1940. Stephen Merchant was the town supervisor and a "master farmer."

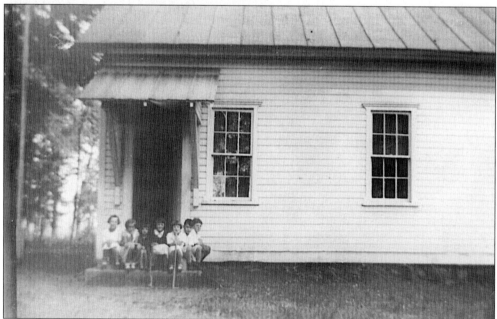

This school was District #4. It was near this spot that Isaac Stow was killed by the British soldiers and Mohawk warriors during the 1780 invasion. Students, from left to right, are Doris Telford, Nellie Christensen, Irene Trieble, Florence Miller, Margaret Christensen, Leonard Trieble, and Richard Christensen. The picture was taken in 1935.

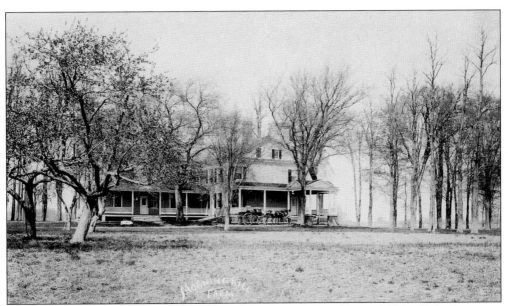

The James Gordon house was known as the Mourning Kill Farm and the Maplewood Stock farm. It stood at 217 Middle Line Road until it was burned in the 1930s. James Gordon's original house was torched in the invasion of 1780. He rebuilt it after the war. George Washington dined here in July 1783. He and his party lost their way from the springs, and when General Washington asked for directions, he was told: "Follow your nose. Any fool knows the way to Gordon's."

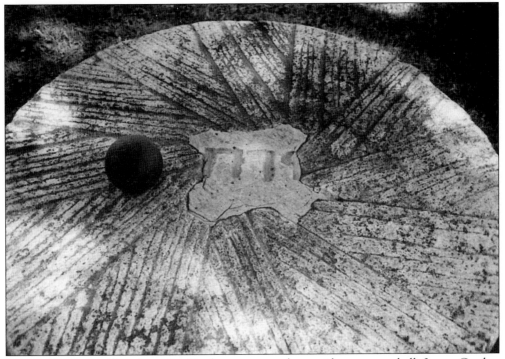

This millstone was found on the Gordon property along with a cannon ball. James Gordon owned gristmills. The stone is dated 1779.

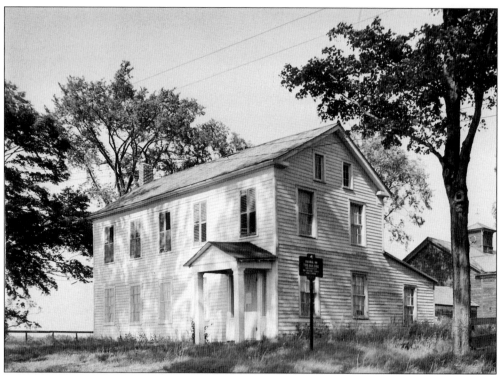

The Saratoga County courthouse was built on the hill on Middle Line Road in 1796. It became the center of legal and political activity. The county jail was part of the complex. Escaping prisoners burned the jail and courthouse in 1816. Across the street from the courthouse, a tavern and inn was established at 288 Middle Line Road. Visiting lawyers and judges stayed at the inn.

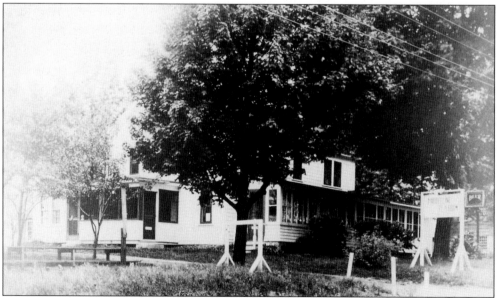

A tearoom was operated at 317 Middle Line Road. There was a picnic grove, and square dances were held here.

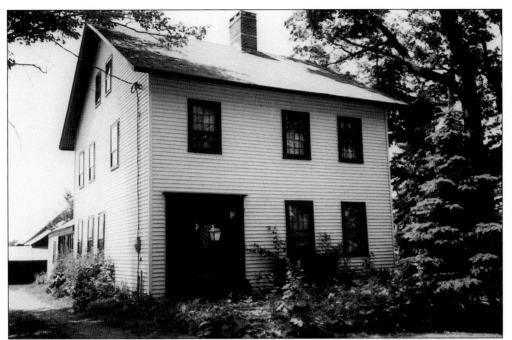

The only structure that survived the invasion of 1780 was the back portion of this house, located at 319 Middle Line Road. Jonathan Filer (or Tiler) saw the lights from burning buildings south of his. He roused his family and ran to hide in the woods. His mother-in-law, "Granny Leake," quelled the flames after the British left. Scorch marks can still be seen in the ceilings of the house. This was where the Mohawk braided torch was found (see page 13).

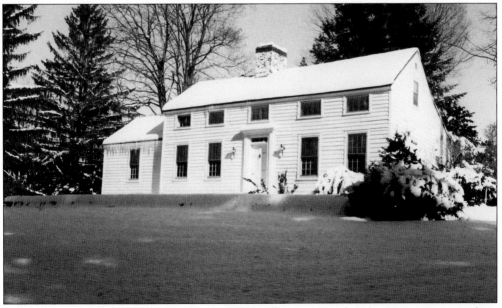

George Scott settled on this property at 386 Middle Line Road. He came to America from Ireland with his wife, Jane, who was the sister of James Gordon. Scott's original house was attacked, and he was left for dead, having been tomahawked by attacking Mohawk warriors. He survived the attack and lived for five more years.

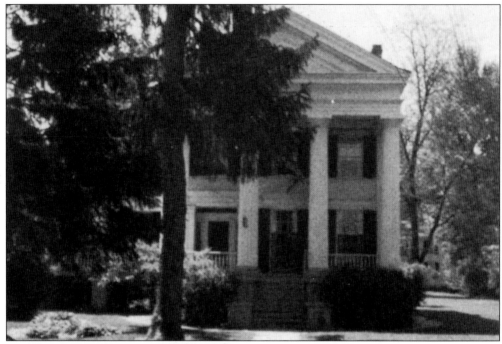

George Gordon Scott lived in this residence on High Street in Ballston Spa. He enjoyed relating the history of his ancestors during the Revolution.

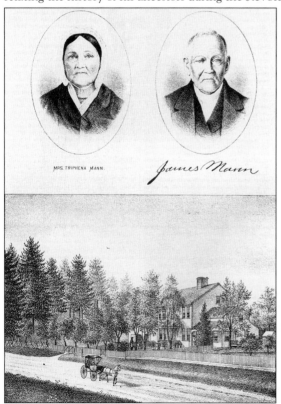

MRS. TRIPHENA MANN.

James Mann

James Mann and his wife, Tryphena, came to Ballston in 1791. His house on Mann Road dates to 1805. This illustration was done by Nathaniel Sylvester in 1878.

Seven
Goode Street

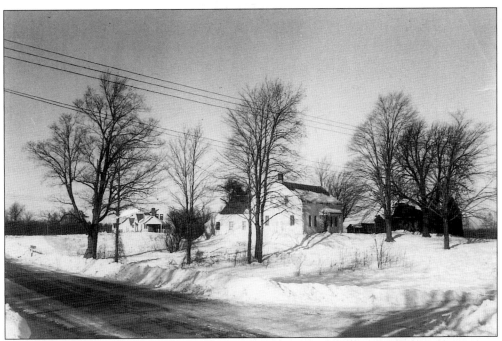

Goode Street derives its name from a WPA project during the Depression. All the stone fences along the road were taken to a stone crusher. The pulverized stone was used on the old dirt road, making this the "good" street. This house, located on the east side at 78 Goode Street, was built c. 1775 by the Sears family. The farm originally contained 70 acres. The house has hand-hewn pine ceiling beams, and one beam is 14 by 20 feet. It was later known as the McKnight farm.

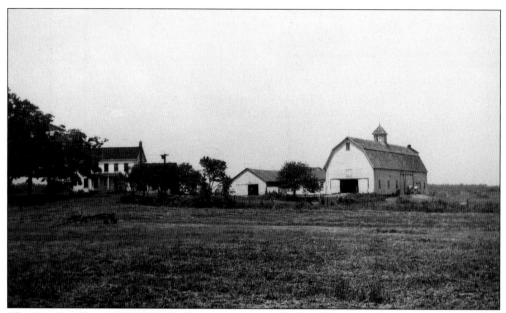

The Garrison farm at 145 Goode Street was originally the Charles and Ann Van Vorst farm. The house was built in 1849 and the farm had 151 acres. David Garrison purchased the farm in 1911. The barn was built at an old-fashioned barn raising. His son, Stan, opened the Burnt Hills Veterinarian Hospital in 1950. He and his wife, Shirley, raised Belgian horses.

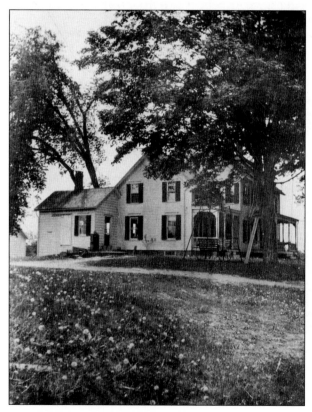

The Stephen Merchant farm is located at 310 Goode Street. It was originally owned by the Quivey family. Stephen Merchant and his wife Alice Morehouse ran a fruit and dairy farm here.

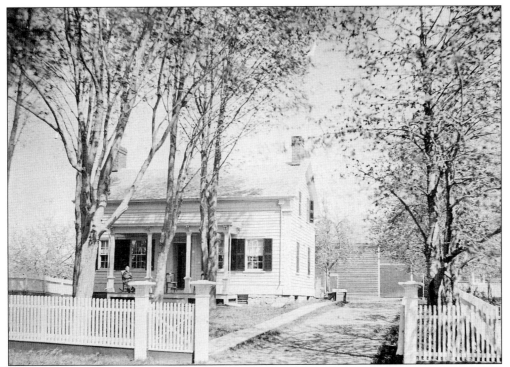

The Red Gate farm was bought by Gerritt Bradt in 1838. Aaron Bradt built the house at 334 Goode Street. Three Bradt sons served in the Civil War in the New York Fourth Artillery. Later, Walter Waite purchased the farm.

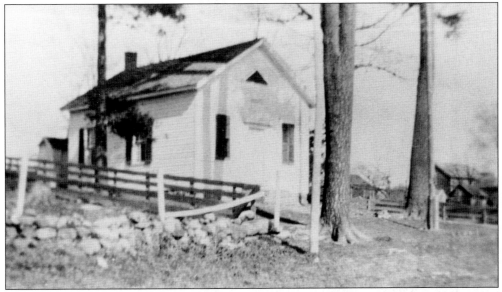

Across the street from the Red Gate farm was a one-room schoolhouse. It burned in 1925, and the students were transported to the Union Free School on Lake Hill Road. Attendance at the one-room schoolhouses was sporadic, as compulsory attendance was not required until 1874. Teachers swept the floors, filled the water pail, and built fires in the stoves. They were allowed to use "the switch" to discipline students.

$100 REWARD!

Stolen on Thursday night, May 2, 1878, from the barn of A. D. Stewart, in the town of Ballston, a pale sorrel

HORSE, with CARRIAGE & HARNESS,

The horse has a very heavy tail, short thin mane, scarcely any fore-top, very heavy body and neck, marked with scratches on both forward feet. Is 15 years old, 15½ hands high, and weighs from 1100 to 1200. The Carriage is a square box, rigged for one or two seats, painted black, with silver-plated band over the dash, and newly tired last summer. Also a light silver-plated Harness, with breast collar, and a head-stall to a heavy harness, and Buffalo Robe marked A. D. S.

$50 reward will be paid for the return of the property, and $50 for the arrest and conviction of the thief.

A. D. STEWART.

Ballston, May 4, 1878.

Horses were farm necessities, and horse thieves were severely punished. The worst crime was murder and the second, stealing a horse. The Saratoga County Society for Detection of Horse Thieves was formed in 1818. It advertised for stolen horses, and the broadsides often included a description of the thief.

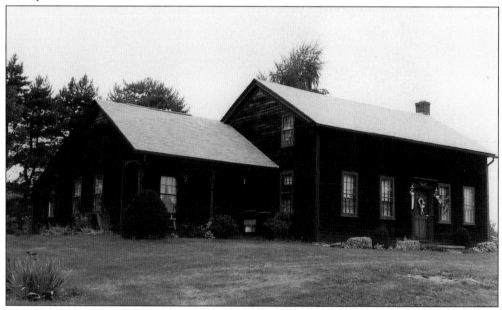

The Tibbets farm was established by 1856. It is located at 359 Goode Street. There are wide plank floors and a Dutch oven, and the cellar walls are fieldstone, 3 feet thick.

John Henry Tibbets was born in 1804 and died in 1882. He was married to Lucy Ann Lacy in 1832 at the Ballston Center Presbyterian Church.

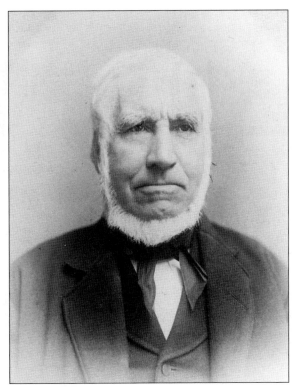

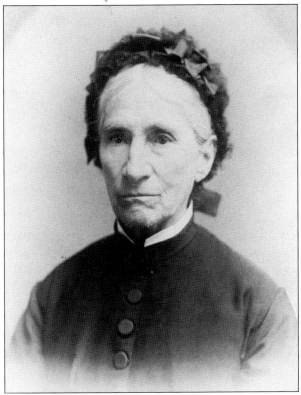

Lucy Ann Lacy Tibbets was the mother of Mary Tibbets, Martha Comstock, and Elizabeth Merchant. Elizabeth was the mother of Stephen H. Merchant. Lucy died in 1893 at the age of 87, and she is buried with her husband in Briggs Cemetery.

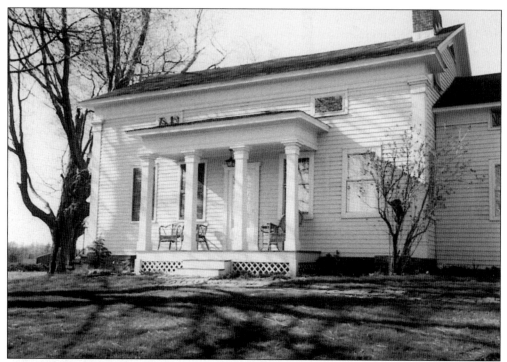

This early home faces south on the west side of Goode Street. The Sears and Crapo families were early owners. It is located at 401 Goode Street.

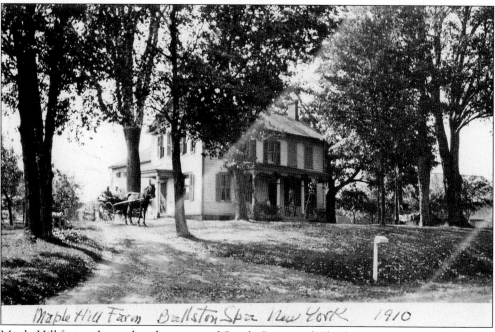

Maple Hill Farm Ballston Spa New York 1910

Maple Hill farm is located at the corner of Goode Street and Charlton Road. The home was in the Larkin family for generations, and the intersection is known as Larkin's Corners. The house was given to Daniel Larkin and his wife, Mary Curtis, in 1852. It was originally one and a half stories and then raised to two stories in 1875.

The house kitty-corner to Maple Hill farm was in the Jennings family for years. An earlier owner was Uriah Gregory. The ratification of the Constitution was celebrated on this property. Thirteen vollies were fired, and an effigy of Benedict Arnold was burned. In this image, Chester Jennings stands on the porch with his grandmother, Hattie Morehouse Jennings, in 1927. She was married to Charles Platt Jennings, who was known to keep over three thousand chickens.

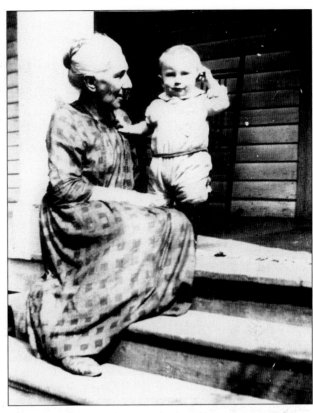

Farther north on the west side of Goode Street was the land cultivated by tenant farmer John Cain. His father, Andrew, was born in Ireland in 1824. John was married to Rachael Miller and is pictured with son Elmer and daughter Emma in 1892. The house burned in 1898.

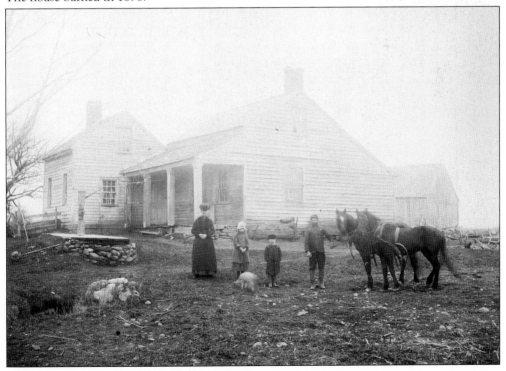

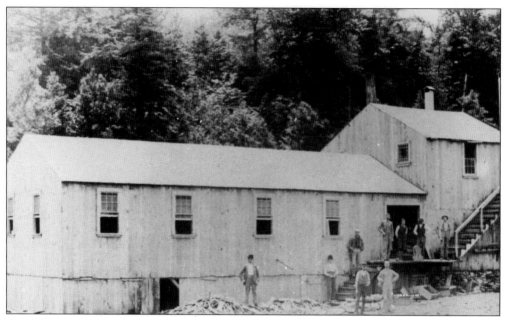

West of Goode Street and on the north side of Charlton Road was the Ballston Cheese factory. It was owned by Robert Davis. Farmers brought their surplus milk to the factory where it was heated to make curds. The excess water was drained off and salt was added. The curd was then pressed into molds lined with cheese cloth. The end product sold for 10¢ a pound.

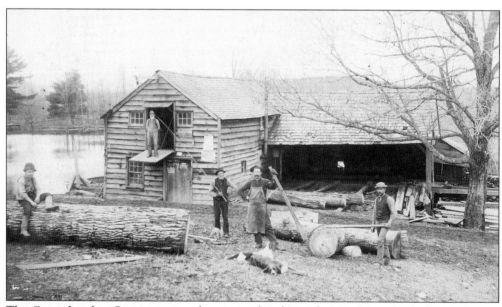

The Curtis Lumber Company was adjacent to the cheese factory. It was built about 1832 by Isaac Curtis and his father-in-law, Nathaniel Booth. The method of operating by waterpower involved a mill pond and dam. Sawing was a slow process carried on during the fall and winter months. Men played cards and gossiped here while waiting for their lumber to be cut. Pictured are Robert David (left and on the log), Mr. Surgess (upstairs), Albert Curtis (with a fishing pole), Will Seeley (with a cant hook), and Elmer Curtis (on far right).

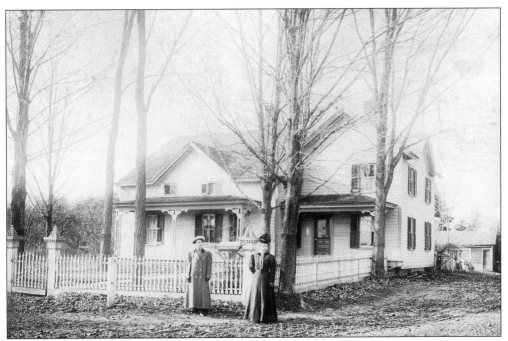

The Curtis house was called Milldale and was west of the sawmill. The house was moved to this location from The Lane and the left portion was original. Mary Larkin Curtis (right), wife of Elmer, is posing here in front of the house with her housekeeper, Hattie Collins (left).

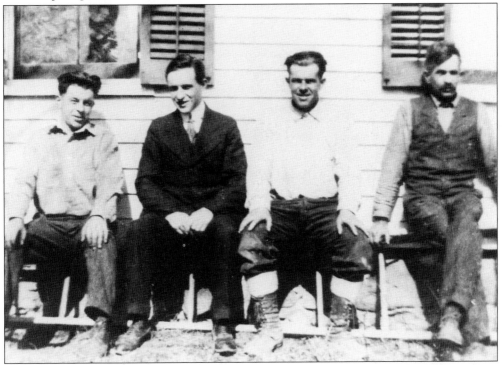

The Curtis men take a break from painting the homestead. From left to right are: Kent, Arthur, Henry, and Elmer Curtis (father).

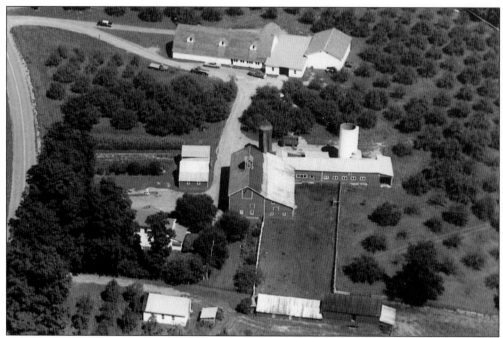

Farther west, at 347 Charlton Road, is the Merchant farm. Stephen Merchant married Edith Van Vorst. The farm annually produced 40,000 bushels of apples, and forty pickers were needed to bring in the crop. The apples were stored in the Dutch-style barn. Macintosh apples were the specialty.

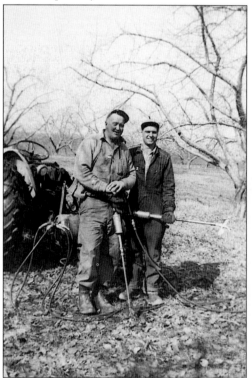

Stephen Merchant is pictured here with his son, Richard, in 1958. They used limb-loppers to trim the trees. Stephen was a fifty-year member of the Ballston Grange and served as the town supervisor from 1946 to 1957.

Eight

Scotch Bush/ Hop City

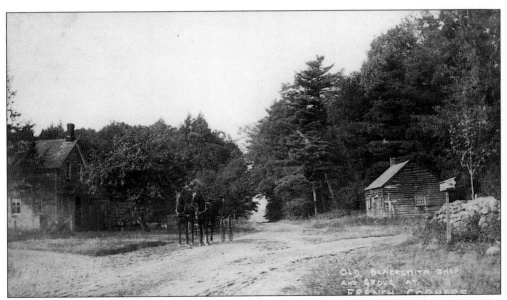

Scotch Bush is named for the Scottish settlement in that area and their hop mills. The blacksmith shop was located at the intersection of Charlton Road and Hop City. This was called French's Corners after the blacksmith Cyrus French.

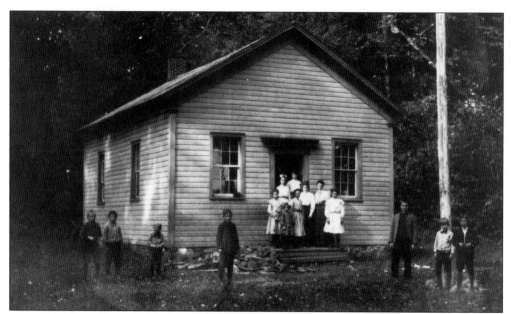

District School #6 was located at the intersection of Scotch Bush and Charlton Road. This picture was taken in 1906.

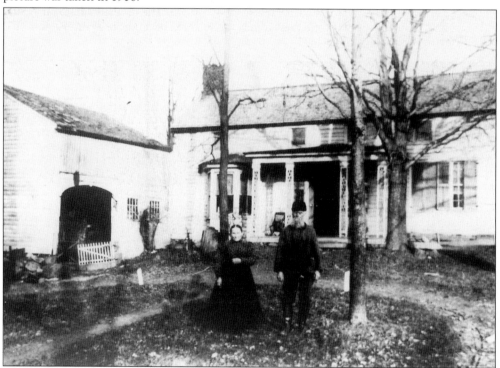

Samuel Rue came to the community in 1814. His saltbox house was built at 250 Hop City Road. A large open-hearth fireplace with a crane was built in the kitchen. Nearby was the "borning room" where his wife Mary cared for her infant, Horton, who was born in 1832. Samuel served as an overseer of the poor. Those in need of clothing, medicines, and lodgings applied to him. He was also responsible for driving the needy out of town.

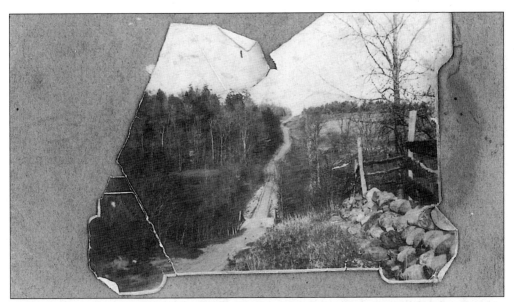

Devils Lane passes east of Hop City Road. The lane derives its name from a ghostly encounter Angus McDearmid, an agnostic who often cursed, had in 1782. One night his cow strayed away, and he went looking for it. At dawn, he spotted a "large monstrous apparition" with a cloven hoof and fiery eyes; the air was filled with the smell of sulphur. The terrified farmer ran home and became a staunch member of the Presbyterian church, and never swore again! He was sure he had seen the devil.

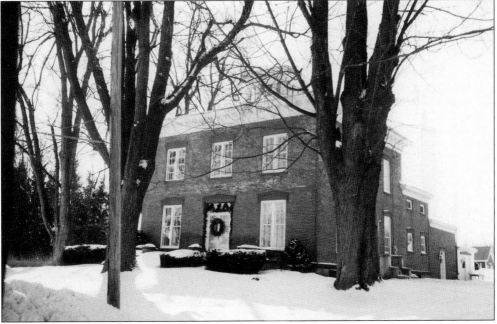

The Brookdale farm is located north of French's Corners, overlooking the Mourningkill Creek. The house was built about 1850 by Horace McKnight. The brick house was the homestead of Horace, his wife Sarah Hayes, and children Horace, Charles, Anna, and John. The house is located at 233 Hop City Road.

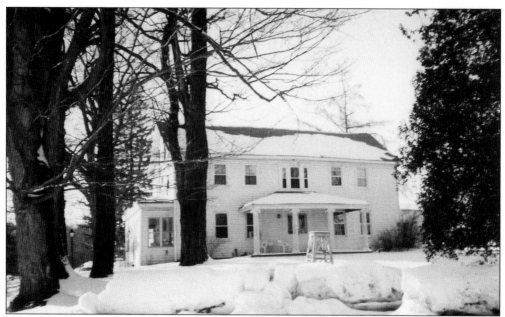

Continuing north on Hop City Road, on the west side is the house known as Willow Marsh Farm, at 343 Hop City Road. Samuel DeForest first settled here in the mid-1780s. Samuel was a Revolutionary War pensioner, who witnessed the Battle of Long Island. He died in 1837 and is buried in the Hubbell Cemetery north of his home. W.S. Curtis purchased the house in 1846, and it has remained in the family for generations. Handmade square nails and a pegged house frame date this house.

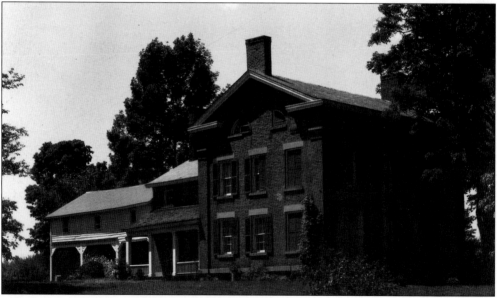

This house is located at 457 Hop City Road. Edmund Jennings settled here c. 1775. The rear portion of the house still contains beams covered by bark. Unlike his Scottish Tory neighbors, Edmund sided with the American patriots. He served in the Albany County militia and galloped off to capture Tories. The front portion was added c. 1820. Portions of the house are 18 inches thick. It was later in the Spears, Barnes, and Kirk families.

Nine
Brookline and East Line

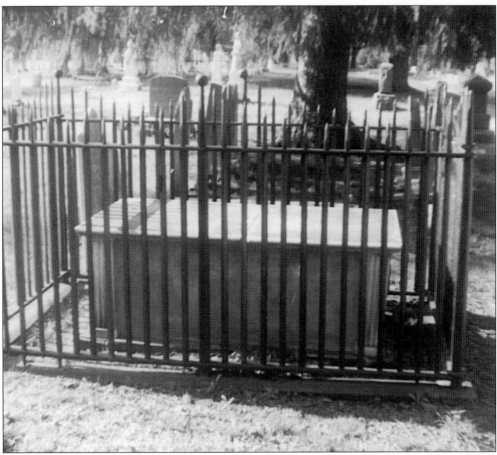

Brookline is named for its location near the Mourningkill Brook, and East Line was just that—the eastern most line of the 5-mile square. Briggs Cemetery is located on the south side of Brookline Road. The first burial was Martha Gordon, the mother of James Gordon, who died in 1775. Captain David Alexander Grant died in 1806. He is buried in the sarcophagus pictured here. He was an influential man in Canada and owned most of Montreal. He was married to Baroness Marie de Longueil.

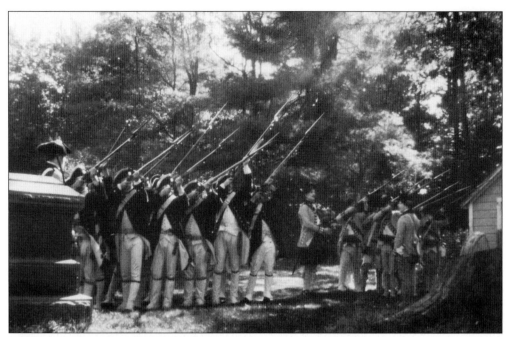

Captain Grant was a member of the 84th Regiment; this regiment was part of the raid on Ballston in 1780. In 1980 the Brigade of the Revolution encamped at Ballston. The 84th, dressed in their emerald green uniforms, fired a salute at Grant's gravesite.

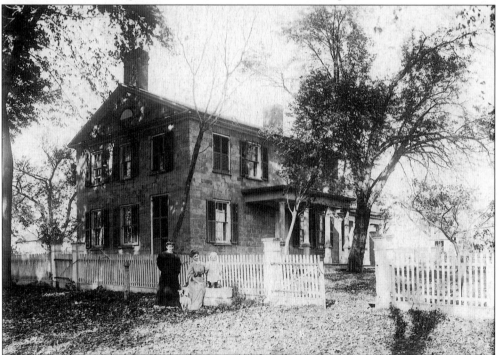

The stone house at 6 Brookline Road was once owned by Edmund Hubbell, who operated a woolen cloth factory. The date 1831 is etched in marble on the house. The seated woman in the picture is Mabel Davey with her child Reita. The woman dressed in black is unknown.

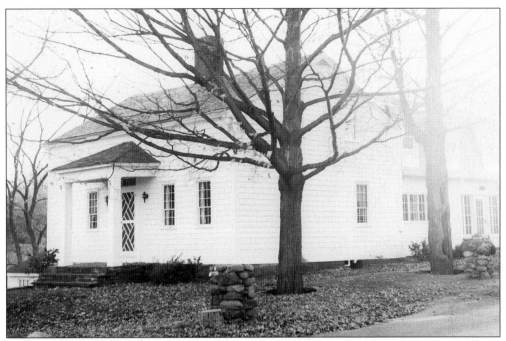

This house at 5 Brookline Road was built *c.* 1800, and it was owned by Sylvester Blood. He was a forge master and ran a trip-hammer to make axes and scythes, using the Mourningkill Creek for waterpower. The Mourningkill name was derived from a Native American battle fought at the creek between the Mohawks and Algonquin tribes; for years, they returned to mourn their dead.

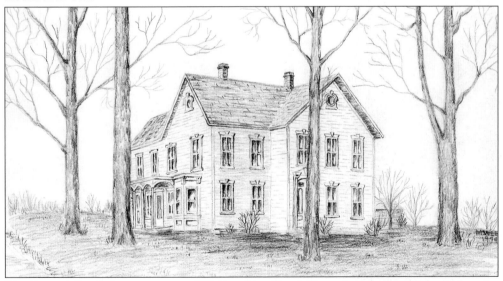

The Samuel Smith house was near 289 East Line Road. Samuel came to Ballston before the Burgoyne campaign. He was a blacksmith and told his neighbors that he would do their blacksmithing if they would go to Stillwater and gather tools from the surrendered Burgoyne camp. They brought back a bellows, vise, and hammer. The house remained in the Smith family for generations. It burned in the 1950s. The drawing of the house was done by Mary Weed.

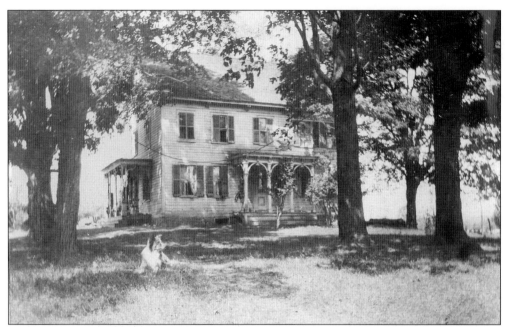

The Joseph Leonard Weed house was owned by Joseph, who was born in 1835. Joseph married Emily Miller, who died in childbirth. His second wife, Mary Beeman, agreed to raise his children if he would raise the roof to make the house two stories high. The house is located at 343 Eastline Road.

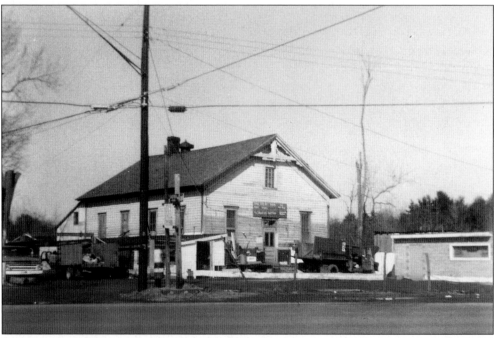

East Line School was a combination of Ballston District #3 and Malta District #8. Students' ages ranged from five to twenty years. It was known as the "toughest school around." The pupils were from Irish and English immigrant families who worked on the area farms. The school once had eight teachers leave in one year!

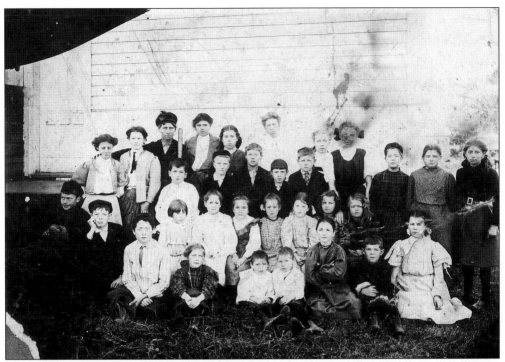

The students of East Line School are shown here. One Halloween, they raised a cow to the roof by using a block and tackle. Bill Hennessey is on the far left of the first row. Bill was known to have nine lives and that he loved each one of them. He served in WW I, WW II, and Korea. He once rode a wild pig out of the Argonne Forest, France

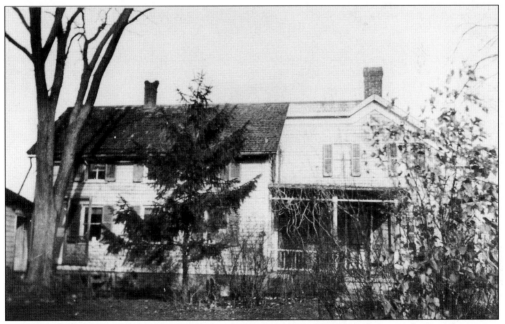

The Elisha Scidmore house is located at 519 East Line Road. Elisha, the son of a Revolutionary War veteran, was born in 1803 and later became a stone mason.

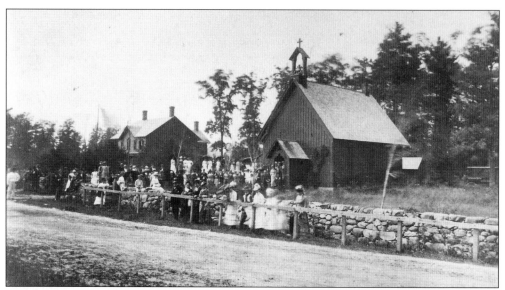

St. John's Episcopal Mission Church, on East Line, was built in 1877. The orphanage, called House of Angels, is on the left. Some sixty orphans died from 1886 to 1891. They are buried in the adjacent St. Christopher Cemetery. The causes of death were "teething" and "marasmus." The orphanage burned in the 1930s.

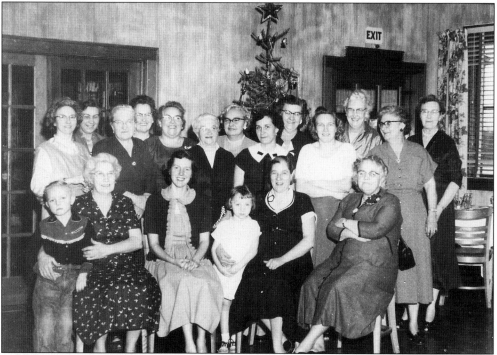

The East Line Ladies Home Bureau posed for this photograph in 1965. From left to right are: (first row) Jimmy Plummer, Nellie Jennings, Louise Schwarz, Caren Plummer, ? Clements, and Lois Comperthwait; (second row) unidentified, Grace Stewart, unidentified, Mrs. Walter Johnson, Dorothy Johnson, Betty Jackson, and Mrs. Brown; (back row) Cleora Baldwin, unidentified, Doris Vedder, ? Whinnery, Carrie Weed, and Edith Bentley.

Ten
Ballston Spa

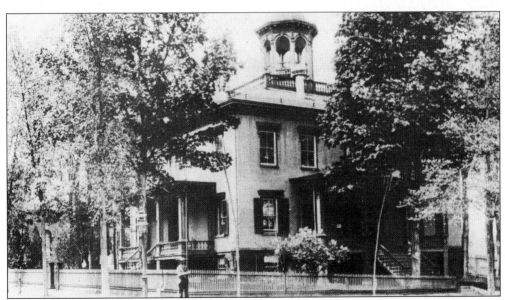

The spas were discovered as springs by the Mohawks, who valued their healing powers. This Saratoga County courthouse was built in 1819 on West High Street in Ballston Spa. It was built for $10,000 and modeled after the one that burned on Court House Hill in 1816. Courts of the county were held here until 1889, when it was demolished.

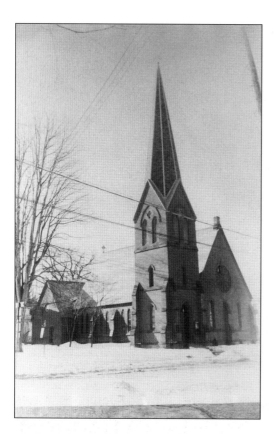

The Christ Episcopal Church was first located at Ballston Center on Middle Line Road. It was built in 1792 and then moved to Ballston Spa in 1817. The cornerstone of this church was laid in 1860.

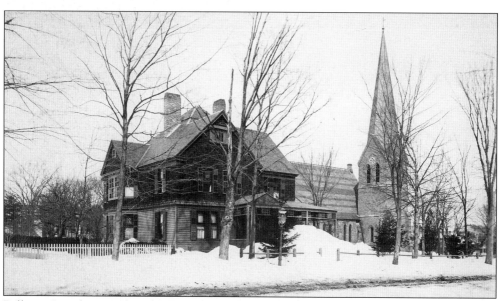

Ballston Spa photographers, such as T.G. Arnold, J.S. Wooley, and Howard Humes, captured moments in time. This wintery scene of Church Avenue was taken *c.* 1900. The earliest photograph, known as the daguerreotype, dates to 1839. This type was followed by Cartes De Visite (1860–1910), cabinet (1875–1910), and postcards (1905–1930).

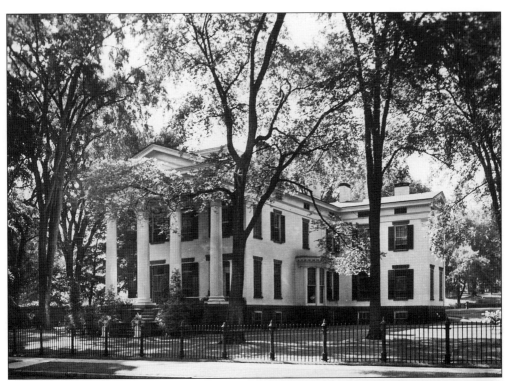

Edward Smith owned an impressive mansion at what is now the Saratoga County complex parking lot. Mr. Smith and his wife, Maude Thompson Smith, had a fishing clearing on Ballston Lake and enjoyed hunting in Georgia. He obtained his wealth from the railroads. The property was purchased in 1946 by Saratoga County.

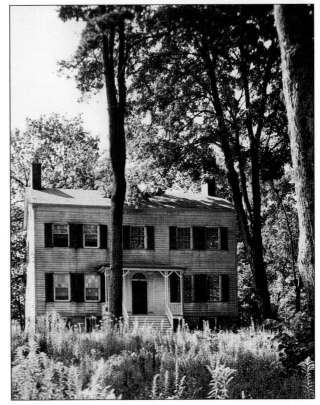

John W. Taylor lived on West High Street. He was born in 1784, and his wife was Jane. They raised nine children here. John Taylor was a member of Congress from 1813 to 1833, Speaker of the House of Representatives from 1821 to 1827, and state senator in 1840. He was an anti-slavery advocate and was visited here by Henry Clay.

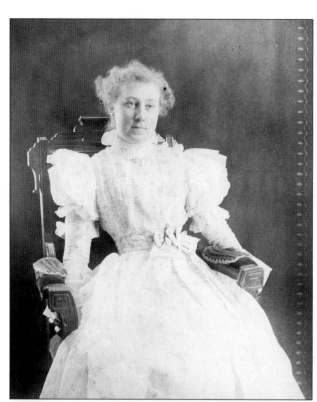

Mae Esmond Young poses here for her wedding picture. She was married in 1891.

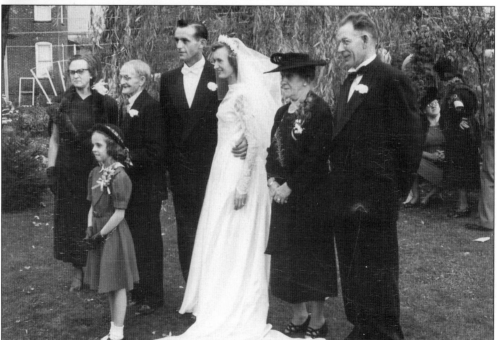

Dick and Vickie Fox posed for this wedding picture in 1949. From left to right are Ellen Winters, mother of the bride; Samuel Davis, Ellen's father; Richard and Vickie Fox; Grace Davis, Samuel's wife; Walter Winters, step-father of the bride; and Judith Winters Cox in front.

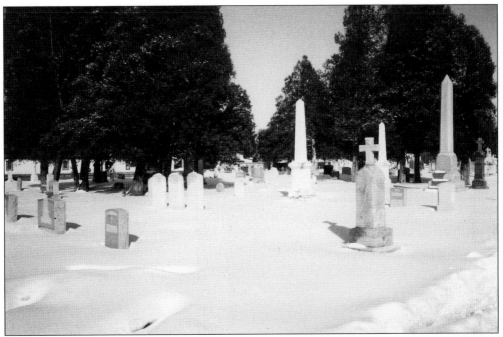

St. Mary's Cemetery is located on Church Street (Route 50). Here, there is a gravestone for Sgt. James Butler Jr., who was killed in the Battle of Little Big Horn, or better known as Custer's Last Stand, in 1876.

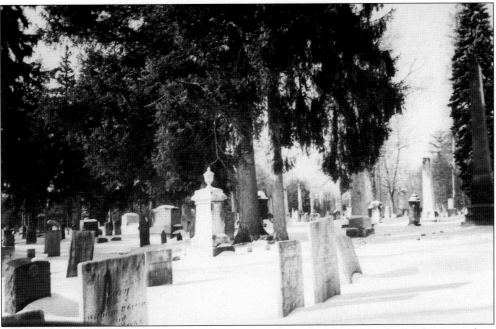

The Ballston Spa Village Cemetery is located on Ballston Avenue. It is the final resting place for many founding families, Civil War veterans, and also "Silent Beckey." Her name was Rebecca Jones, and in 1884, she was jailed for refusing to give evidence in a $7-million estate contest. She was a woman who became famous by keeping her mouth shut!

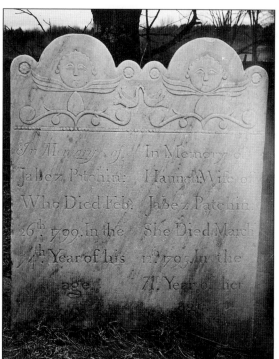

This gravestone is located on Middle Line Road. Jabez Patchin died in 1799, at age 74. His wife's stone is engraved, "Hannah," who died in 1795 at age 71. The angels represent heavenly guides, and the doves symbolize purity.

Baseball has been an integral part of Ballston Spa's heritage, given that Abner Doubleday was born in the village; Mr. Doubleday is the acknowledged inventor of the game. Pictured here in 1930, from left to right, are: (front row) Fred Martin, Peter Solotruck, Alex Johnson, and Clarence Tuper; (second row) Bill Fitzgerald, Frank Thomas, Joe Kvasnack, Joe Bush, Ernie Estes, and unidentified; (back row) Bill Van Dyke, George McDonough, Theodore Peck, Joe Gorman, Earl Guertin, and coach Ward Jones.

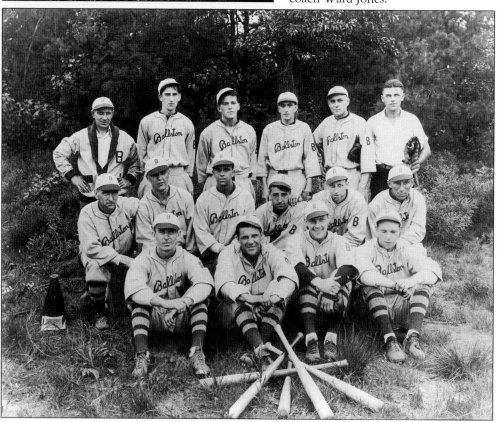

Henry Grose was born in 1816. He was a doctor, lawyer, owner and editor of the *Ballston Journal*, and chaplain of the 29th Regiment. He was a Baptist minister and supplied the pulpit at Burnt Hills for several months.

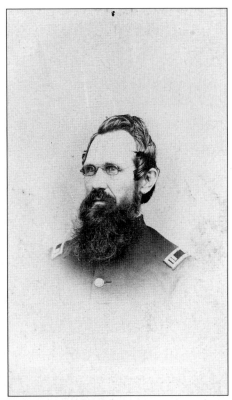

Young soldiers pose here in front of Christ Episcopal Church.

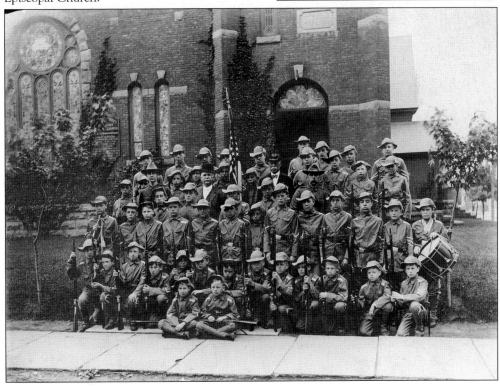

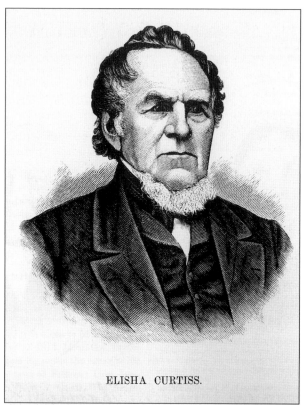

ELISHA CURTISS.

Elisha Curtiss was instrumental in the building of the Erie Canal and Schenectady railroad. He married Betsey Waterman, the daughter of Asa Waterman. After her death, he married her sister, Belinda. This print was taken from Nathaniel Sylvester's *History of Saratoga County* (1878).

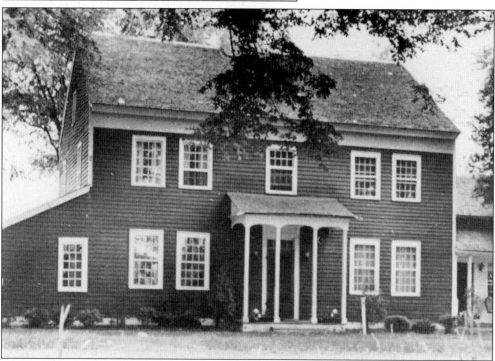

The Mann homestead was built by James Mann in 1805.

VISIT THE NATIONAL BOTTLE MUSEUM

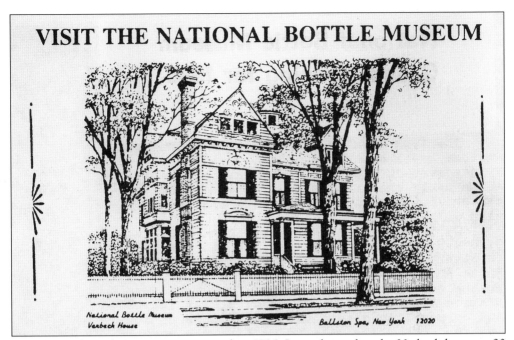

National Bottle Museum
Verbeck House

Ballston Spa, New York 12020

The National Bottle Museum was opened in 1986. It was located at the Verbeck house at 20 Church Avenue. It housed collections of milk bottles, jelly jars, and ink wells.

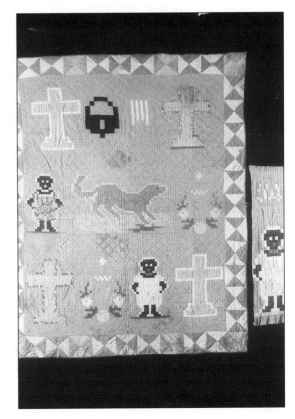

This quilt was found in a trunk at 459 Charlton Road. It is large enough for a double bed and was made *c*. 1870. The symbols represent religious orientation and freedom. It is believed that an African American stitched the quilt.

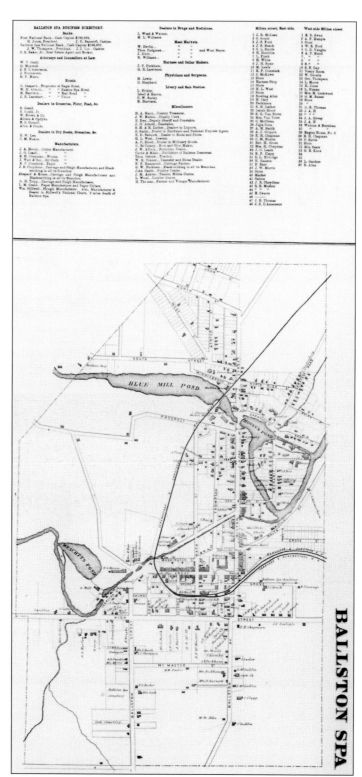

Pictured here is a village map dated 1866.

Eleven
Here and There

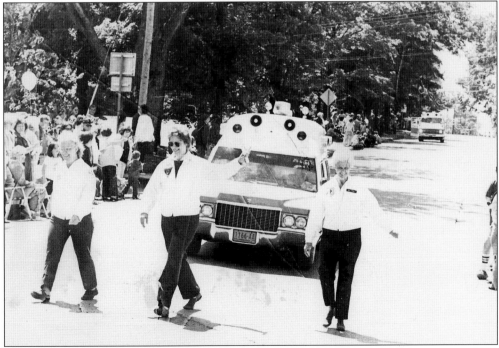

The Ballston Lake Ambulance Squad was organized in 1951. The first ambulance was a 1939 secondhand La Salle. Pictured here in 1976 are, from left to right, Blanche Hart, Judy Streever, and Bev Strott.

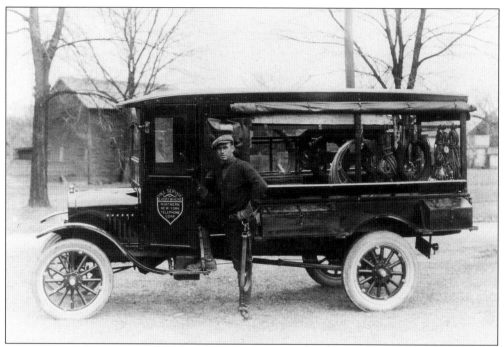

Telephones came to Ballston in the 1890s. This lineman poses for a 1924 photograph. Most houses had telephones by then.

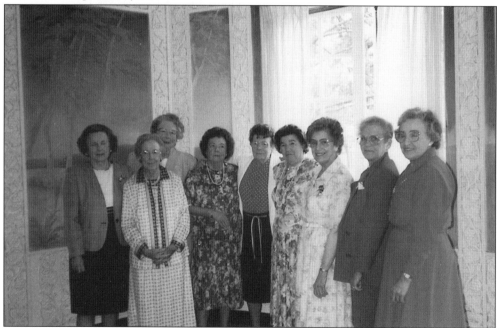

The Burnt Hills-Ballston Lake Women's Club was organized in 1949. The purpose was to promote civic and social improvements. They sponsor scholarships, provide hearing tests for children, and landscape community facilities. Some of the members are, from left to right: Mary Hannon, Florence White, Grace Jones, Terry Shea, Jean Anderson, Toly Svolos, Virginia Wolski, Shirley Webster, and Dot Hopkinson.

114

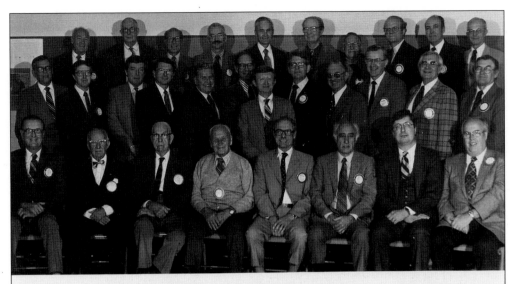

BURNT HILLS - BALLSTON LAKE ROTARY CLUB

First Row: Bill Sewell, Frank Stevens, Earl Smith, Alex Stewart, Morris Eiland
Burt Coons, Bob Van Vranken, Curt Barber
Second Row:Ed Freiburghouse, Jim Smith, Skip Pott, John Gay, Bob Sawyer,
Art Mengel, Mahlon Clifford, Clarence Linder, Carl Shopmyer,
Dick O'Rourke, Mike Nazar, Walt Grattidge
Third Row: Bill Bennett, Bill Dotter, Earl Wilmot, Len Porter, Dick Carlson,
Walt Kessler, Jim Burnett, Ed Warren, Chuck McLoughlin, Al Fritz
Missing From Picture: Jack Ahern, Dick Boord, Chet Clarke, Ron Conklin,
George Fridholm, Stan Garrison, Bill McClary, Gerry Smallwood,
Harold Townley, Joe Walsh, Jack Wolfe, Pat Oles   May 10, 1983

The BH-BL Rotary Club was chartered in 1951. Their motto is "Service Above Self." Some of their projects include sponsoring foreign exchange students, cleaning cemeteries, improving Clover Patch Club, and providing scholarships.

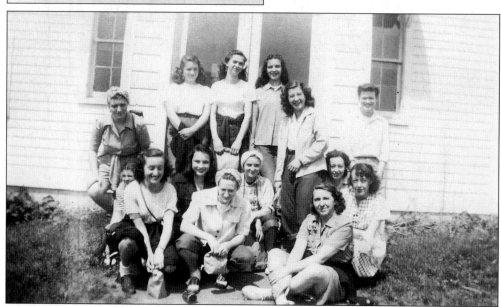

Esther Kennedy
Wealthy Hubbs
Ann Roads
Esther Roads
Emma Brooks
Clarrissa Brooks
Arzela Hollister
Harriet Hollister
Nancy Milard
Sarah Ann Sheldon
Mary Covey
Esther Schauber
Matilda Chatsey
Betsey Bently
Huldah Lion
Lavina Lion
Cynthia Bancker Tutoress
Halfmoon 1821

Young ladies once stitched samplers to show their skill in needlework. This embroidery was done by the students of the Schauber Hill School. Chester Arthur, twenty-first president of the United States, taught at this school *c.* 1850.

Mrs. Claire Parkis organized the Girl Scouts in 1936. This photograph was taken in 1947. From left to right are: (front row) Dot Bates, Virginia Kilts, and Connie Falconer; (second row) Sandy Breitbeck, Katherine Jones, Evelyn Dadez, Sybil Seibert, and unidentified; (third row) Joan Falconer, Bev Stephenson, and unidentified; (back row) Fran Nessle, Bev Bates, and Pat McPhilomy.

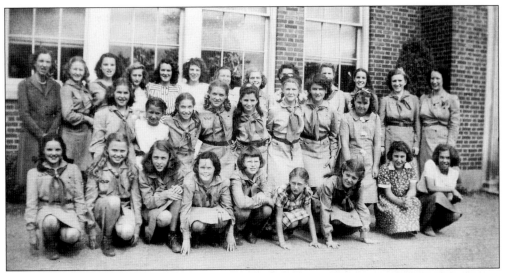

This 1943 photograph shows, from left to right: (front row) Nancy Seelye, Carole Piercy, Barbara Murnane, Virginia Adams, Pam Warner, Barbara Rowledge, Eleanor Cunningham, and unidentified; (second row) unidentified, Betsy Hodgman, unidentified, Rebecca Rowledge, Kathleen Mooney, Gwendolyn Himmelwright, Florence Varone, and unidentified; (back row) leader Betty Hodgman, Sarah Hodgman, Katherine Jones, Virginia Kilts, Florence Stewart, Connie D'Anazio, unidentified, Lanetta Heckler, unidentified, unidentified, Elizabeth Seelye, Joan Falconer, and leader Marian Van Dorn.

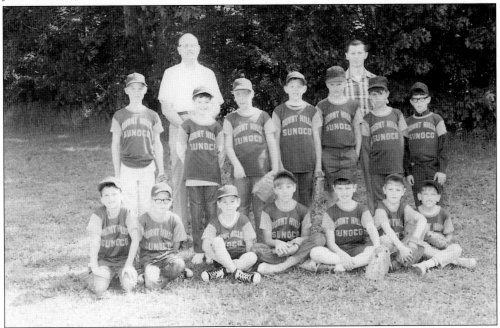

Little League baseball teams have been important for young boys and girls. This 1969 photograph shows, from left to right: (front row) Don Fabini, Brad Oudt, Nick Shear, Dave Metz, Greg Fridholm, Chris Fridholm, and Jeff Fontaine; (back row) Steve Youmans, Bill Korman, Chris Eberle, Pete Curren, Jerry Keeler, Kurt Daubenschmidt, and Mike Brewster. Coaches were Mr. Fridholm and Mr. Korman.

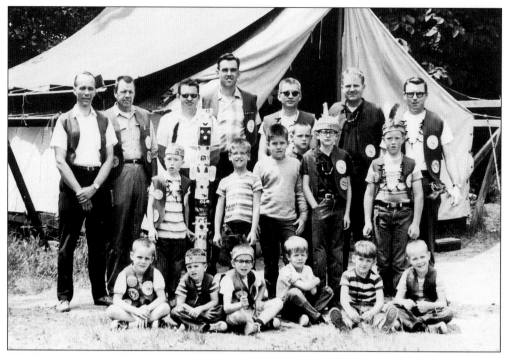

Y-Indian Guides posed for this image in 1968. From left to right are: (front row) Jack Gribben, Tony Rohrmeier, Brad Oudt, Chris Hallgren, Steve Porter, and Andy Gessner; (second row) Bob Coll, Mark Porter, Allan Porter, Bruce Gribben, Will Hallgren, and Chris Coll; (back row) fathers Bob Gessner, Al Oudt, Tony Rohrmeier, Dick Gribben, Len Porter, Doug Hallgren, and Mr. Coll.

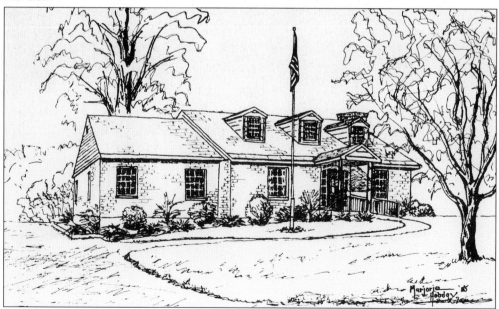

The BH-BL Community Library was organized in 1952, the result of a combined project of the Women's Club and Rotary Club. The following year, Jesse Townley, wife of Earl, donated the land. The library was dedicated in 1958. This drawing was done by Marjorie Hobday.

Twelve
Ballston Celebrations

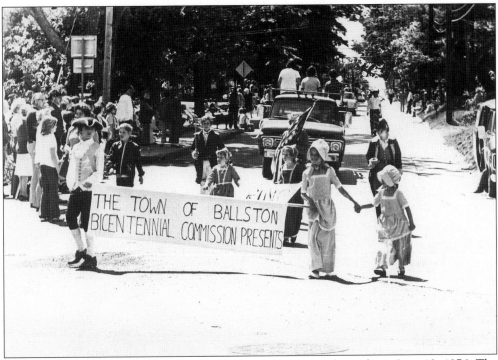

John, Beth, and Maggie Briaddy led the National Bicentennial parade on June 12, 1976. The theme of the event was "Ring the Bells." Square dancing and a fireworks display followed.

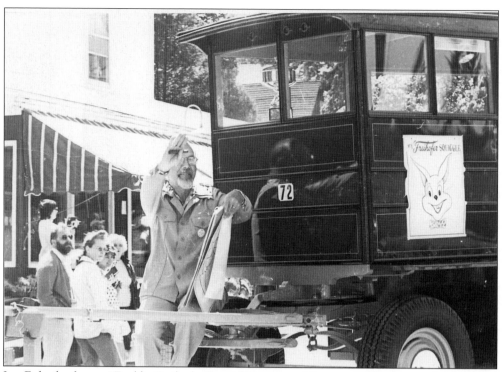

Jim Fisk, the former "Freddie Freihofer," was driven on a delivery truck in the parade.

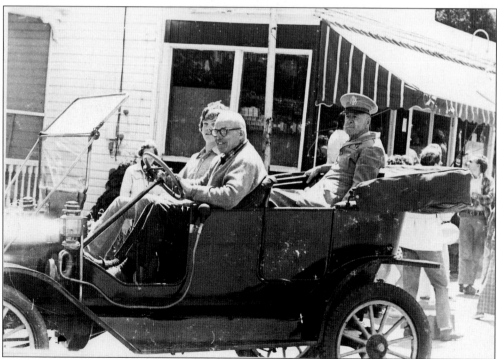

Alan Collyer drove Lieutenant Colonel Lawrence Dussault in the parade. He served in World War II and the Korean conflict. He saw action in Panama, Australia, and France.

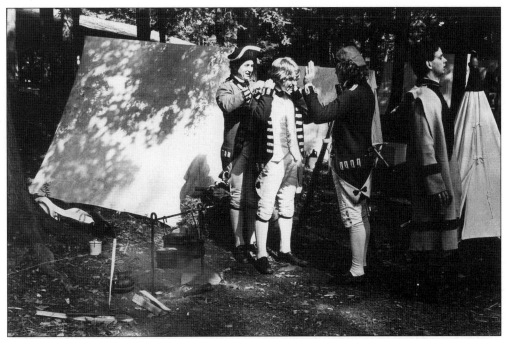

On September 27 and 28, 1980, the American Brigade of the Revolution visited Ballston to commemorate the 200th anniversary of the British invasion. There were units from each of the thirteen original colonies and two regiments from Canada. Over two hundred men, women, and children re-enacted the invasion of Middle Line Road. The Brigade used exact replicas of uniforms and musketry.

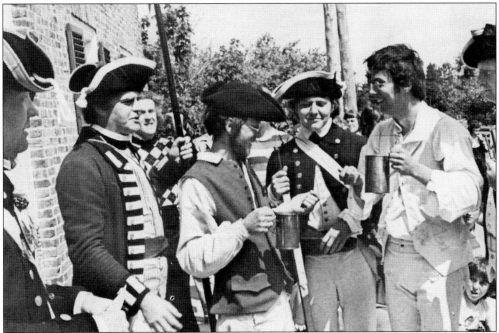

The American Brigade reenacted a soldier's acceptance of the King's shilling. If a shilling was slipped into a man's tankard of ale, his life and loyalty belonged to the King of England.

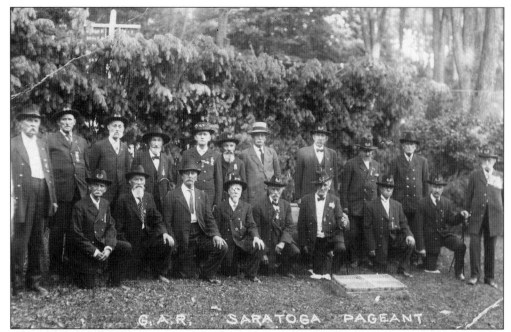

Civil War veterans held a national encampment at Saratoga in September of 1907. Standing in the second row, fourth from the left, is Andrew Miller from Ballston. He served in the 77th New York Volunteers. The regiment saw action at Fredericksburg, Spottsylvania, and the Battles of the Wilderness.

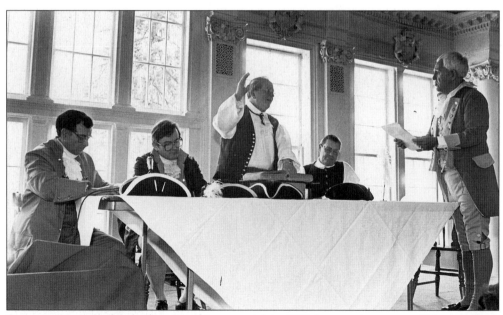

Saratoga County celebrated its own bicentennial in 1991 because it was set off from Albany County in 1791. The first county board of supervisor's meeting was re-enacted as Raymond Callanan (standing) portrayed Beriah Palmer, the county's first supervisor. He was sworn in by David Rathbone, who portrayed Dirck Swart, Justice of the Peace.

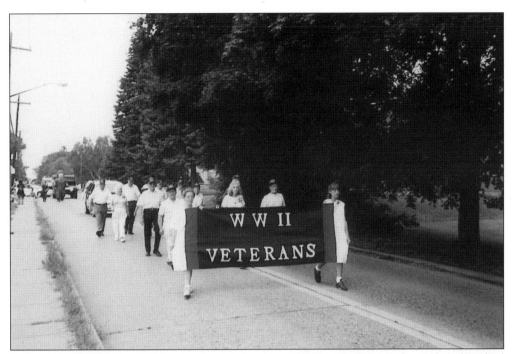

Ballston celebrated the 50th anniversary of victory in WW II. The names of over three hundred Ballston soldiers who fought in World War II were listed in a commemorative book. They were in the Normandy Invasion and the death march of Bataan. One of the veterans listed drove the first American tank into Berlin.

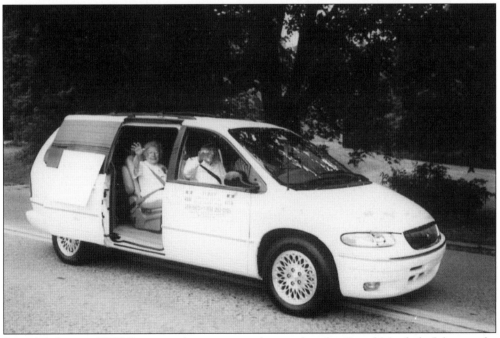

Stan Ashdown, a WW II veteran (passenger seat), served as the Grand Marshal of the parade. He was driven with his wife, Peg (backseat), at the head of the parade.

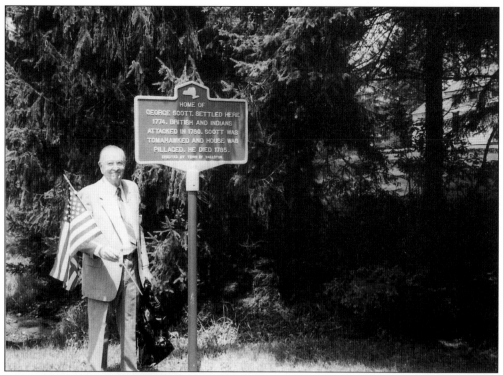

Heritage Day is held on a yearly basis. It is at this time that new New York State historic markers are unveiled. Bill Sewell, supervisor from 1978 until 1987, unveiled and dedicated the marker at the George Scott house.

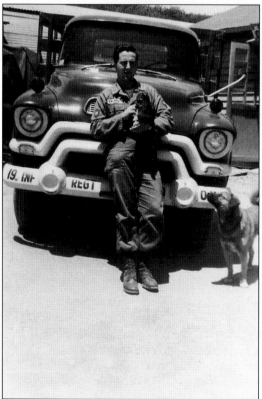

Ray Callanan is a veteran of the Korean conflict and has served as town supervisor since 1988. In 1995 the bicycle path was dedicated to all veterans.

Thirteen

A Last Look at the Lake

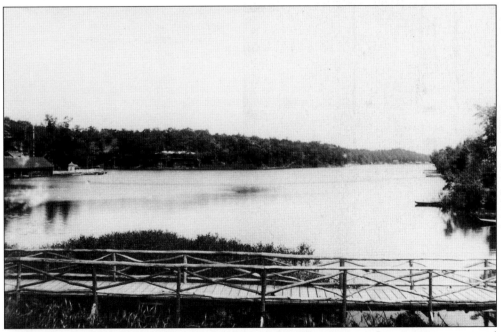

The causeway was on the south end of Ballston Lake. There were a few summer camps and fishing clearances. Wooden cribs (like cages) were used so that the very young and the very old could take dips into the water.

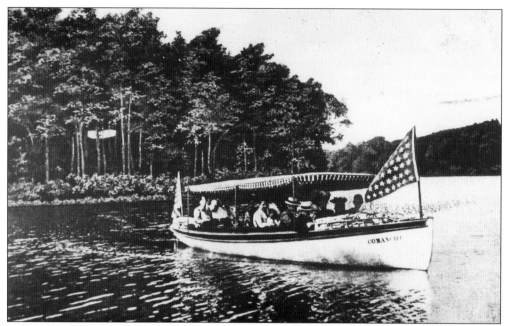

The *Comanche* steamboat provided summer enjoyment for many people on Ballston Lake.

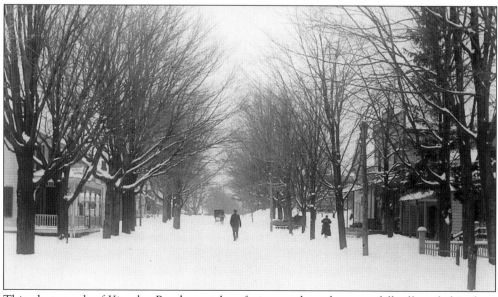

This photograph of Kingsley Road was taken facing south as the townsfolk all settled in for a long winter's nap.

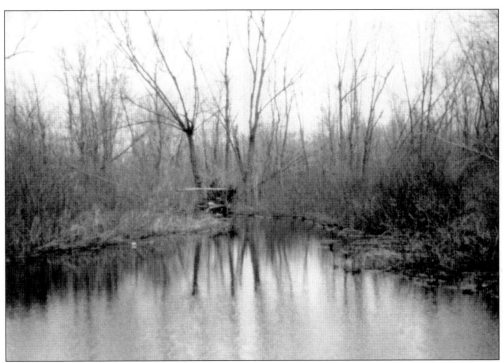

This view was taken from the outlet facing north. The Mohawk spring is located near this site, and the Mohawks maintained a central fire pit on the east side of the lake. A town fishing pier, constructed by the Highway Department, is on Outlet Road.

Acknowledgments

History is a strange study. It is always one step beyond our grasp. By using photographs, we can catch a glimpse. A sincere thank you is extended to the following people who contributed pictures:

Mary and Bill Egan, Jack and Lenore Reber, Muriel Swatling, Peter Jensen, John Kovacik, Penny Heritage, Brad Callahan, Millard Rue, Cheryl Parkhurst, Harold Townley, Esther Sage, Bill Short, Nancy Murtlow, Reverend Beth Dewey, Bud Stevens, Marjorie Hobday, Ed Keeler, George Kline, Dave Skelly, Loris Sawchuk, Lucy Doriguzzi, Anna Horstman, Dorothy Hopkinson, Chester Jennings, Chris Morely, Marriam Ellsworth, Connie Callanan, Zilphia Kirk, Joan Hallgren, Karen Campola, Jeff Pearce, Art Mengel, Judy Warren, Harvey Handel, Ruth and Glen Center, Royal Arnold, Rachael Clothier, Stan Garrison, Jim Hall, Robert Curtis, Merl Reynolds, Vickie and Dick Fox, John Lange, Donald Feeney, Genevieve Van Vranken, Rodney Jackson, Nancy Voehringer, Pat and Charles Merriam, Joyce and Bob Boice, Barbara Olsen, Florence Breitbeck, Bev Oudt, Bob McBroom, Anna Thorpe, Mary Dunn, Maggie Davis, Bernice Knight, Janet and Don Waite, Anita Wagner, Edward Sutphen, Jack Randall, Ruth Roerig, George Peck, Kay and Richard Merchant, Jack Westbrook, David Trombley, Connie Falconer, Debbie Drake, and Anna and Richard Horstman.

Much appreciation is extended to John Scherer, Town of Clifton Park Historian; Photo Images; and Ballston Town Board for their support. All of these people have made this nostalgic tour around the Town of Ballston possible, especially my husband, Jim.